The New Commune-ist Manifesto

Workers of the world, it really is time to unite!

by

Ernesto (Ernie) Raj Peshkov-Chow

(An avatar of the international working class)

First printing July 2013

Cover by Working Design

Printed and bound in Canada by Marquis Printing

A co-publication of

RED Publishing

2736 Cambridge Street

Vancouver, British Columbia V5K 1L7 and

Fernwood Publishing

32 Oceanvista Lane, Black Point, Nova Scotia, B0J 1B0

and 748 Broadway Avenue, Winnipeg, Manitoba, R3G 0X3

www.fernwoodpublishing.ca

Le Conseil des Arts | The Canada Council du Canada | for the Arts   Canadian Heritage   Patrimoine canadien   NOVA SCOTIA   Manitoba

Fernwood Publishing Company Limited gratefully acknowledges the financial support of the Government of Canada through the Canada Book Fund and the Canada Council for the Arts, the Nova Scotia Department of Communities, Culture and Heritage, the Manitoba Department of Culture, Heritage and Tourism under the Manitoba Publishers Marketing Assistance Program and the Province of Manitoba, through the Book Publishing Tax Credit, for our publishing program.

Library and Archives Canada Cataloguing in Publication

Peshkov-Chow, Ernesto Raj, 1953-, author

  The new commune-ist manifesto : workers of the world, it really is time to unite! / by Ernesto (Ernie) Raj Peshkov-Chow.

Includes English translation of Manifest der Kommunistischen Partei by Samuel Moore, first published 1888.

Includes bibliographical references and index.

Co-published by: RED Publishing.

ISBN 978-1-55266-589-3 (pbk.)

  1. Marx, Karl, 1818-1883. Manifest der Kommunistischen Partei. 2. Communism. 3. Socialism. 4. Sustainable development. 5. Environmental economics. I. Marx, Karl, 1818-1883. Manifest der Kommunistischen Partei. English. II. Title. III. Title: New communeist manifesto.

HX39.5.P48 2013   335.4'22   C2013-903054-9

Table of Contents

Preface

This book began with a question. If Karl Marx were alive today and was asked to write a new edition of the Communist Manifesto, how would it be different from the original composed in 1848 by him and Friedrich Engels?

After numerous false starts and much consideration, especially about who Karl Marx was and would still be, the question changed. How to choose the right author? If Marx could have been asked to choose someone to update his work 130 years after he died what sort of criteria would he have suggested? A worker who is also a well-read intellectual; an internationalist, who can see beyond narrow ethnic or cultural boundaries; someone who has dedicated his life to the betterment and empowerment of the international working class; someone serious but with a sense of humor.

Next came the realization that I knew the perfect author for the project. He had already written one book for me, *The Great Multicultural North — A Canadian Primer,* which is about the potential for creating a post-ethnic, democratic, internationalist nationalism in the Great White North. Ernesto (Ernie) Raj Peshkov-Chow has been a union and political activist all his life. He is what certain people would call an "organic intellectual" or, to put it in plain language, he learned about Marxism through conversations and reading books to help make sense of the struggles he was engaged in. These ranged from strikes to elections, union servicing and international solidarity. He came from a left-wing family, so has a strong sense of working-class history. Equally as important is his pan-ethnic background.

Ernie's great-great-grandfather was Walter Chow, born in Barkerville, during the B.C. gold rush in 1861, the son of a Chinese miner from California and a Métis whorehouse owner from Fort

St. James. He married the daughter of a freed American slave, who immigrated to Salt Spring Island in the 1850s, and a Hawaiian man, whose family had been brought to North America as indentured servants in the 1840s by the Hudson's Bay Company. Their first-born son, John Chow, married the daughter of Russian-Finnish anarchists whose son was Ernie's grandfather Leo Peshkov-Chow. In 1931 Leo married Surinder Ghopal and two months later Ernie's father Raj was born. Raj got together with Julietta Martinez, the daughter of a Spanish Civil War veteran married to an Arab-Berber born in Morocco and they became the parents of our author.

Or at least that's the story I was told.

Perhaps because of his heritage Ernie finds the idea of "race" to be ridiculous. However he does believe that racism is very real and that its legacy and current incarnations must be overcome.

Hold on, you might think, Ernie is too perfect to be real. And in one sense you'd be right. He is a projection — an avatar — of the international working class as imagined by me. Of course, the creator of an avatar is present in his creation. Ernie is both me and transcends me. I too have been a working-class activist in one fashion or another all my life, but not as much as Ernie. I too come from an indeterminate ethnic background, but not as indeterminate as Ernie. I too have read and talked about Marxism for just about all my life, but not as much as Ernie. Not unlike an actor following the "Method" school I have looked within in an attempt to create a character who is an ideal but nonetheless rooted in reality. That ideal is the consciousness of the common interests of a pan-ethnic, international working class, the majority of humanity, who Marx wrote would one day end capitalist rule and create a classless society organized around the principle: From each according to their ability, to each according to their need.

My brother Al Engler, his partner Jean Rands, and my son Yves Engler also played significant roles in helping Ernie write this update of the Communist Manifesto. Al, who has written two books about Marxism and economic democracy, has been an active participant in the union movement and broader class struggle for over 50 years. Jean has been a feminist union activist and organizer for as long. Yves, author of seven books about the environment and Canadian foreign policy, brought the viewpoint of the next generation of left-wingers. I am currently a full-time elected local union officer and have also served as a shop steward, chief steward and organizer at the local and national union level.

Ernie was also served by the criticisms and suggestions of former fellow East Vancouver resident, Mike Leibowitz, who is a Marxist scholar of some reknown. Ernie has never held that against him and in fact considers Mike a comrade in the struggle to make a better world.

Regardless of whether you agree or disagree with what follows, the hope is that you will open your mind to the possibilities of change. Too often when we get upset with what our political and economic system delivers, the answer to our complaints is: "That's just the way things are. There's no alternative." But that's not true. Below is an alternative.

The original Communist Manifesto is included as an appendix (From the online edition on the Marxism Page — www. anu.edu.au/polsci/marx/marx.htm) so that, if you like, you can compare and contrast, agree or disagree with our changes.

Gary Engler, June 2013

Introduction

A Conversation with Ernie

The following is an edited version of conversations that Gary Engler and Ernie Peshkov-Chow had about the New Communist Manifesto before it was written.

GE — Do you consider yourself a Marxist?

EPC — I think Karl Marx was a great thinker who was on the side of common people. Every person who wants to improve the lives of working people and get rid of capitalism should read and carefully consider what he wrote.

GE — Did you ever study Marxism?

EPC — No, but I know a lot from hanging around with communists of all brands, especially back in the 70s when there was a Trotskyist arguing with a Maoist of one sort or another on every corner. Plus I've read everything he wrote and a hell of a lot more that other people wrote about him. Some people collect baseball cards, I collect and read left-wing books.

GE — What do you like and not like about Marx?

EPC — Well, some of his stuff is hard to read until you get used to it. The single best thing is that he forces you to look at the big picture. That's what he was all about. Kind of like an ecologist studying the whole forest, rather than just looking at a single tree. Marx teaches you to think about the interconnections, the totality, so you get a better idea of how things really work.

GE — How would you define a Marxist?

EPC — I wouldn't. The truth is that people calling themselves Marxists do not agree on what it means to be a Marxist. Entire political and academic careers have been built around differing interpretations. Sometimes these "Marxists" sound more like religious fundamentalists arguing over the Word of God.

GE — What do you think of that kind of Marxist?

EPC — Well, let's just say this new Communist Manifesto will not be written for that kind of Marxist. In fact it won't be written for self-identified Marxists at all, although maybe they'll want to read it. This new Communist Manifesto will be written for working people who believe we should and can make a better world. It will be written for the employed and unemployed, students and seniors who are looking for an alternative to the inequality of capitalism, and for a way out of the environmental destruction that comes from an economic system demanding ever more profit and growth. It will be written for the victims of a system that uses violence, racism, sexism and other divide-and-conquer techniques to maintain and expand its power. It will be written for the victims of a system that uses brainwashing (also called marketing) to expand its power through ever more addictions to various forms of consumption. It will be written for those victims who no longer want to be victims.

GE — You'll be writing for the working class?

EPC — Exactly. The same basic audience that Marx and Engels wrote for in 1848 and there were no Marxists around then.

GE — Do you agree with all the stuff that Engels and Marx wrote in 1848?

EPC — Times have changed, human relations and social entitlements have changed, science and technology have advanced.

GE — You know that some people are sensitive about changing the original?

EPC — I never read anything by Karl or Freddy to suggest they were the least bit religious, let alone prophets setting in stone the Word of the Communist God.

GE — Meaning?

EPC — Meaning they were reality-based thinkers. They followed evidence. They learned from history. They used the scientific method — probably too crudely — and changed their minds when evidence proved them wrong. Like when Marx by the 1870s was attacking the "iron law of wages" even though something like it was in the orginal Manifesto.

GE — So where they write that workers will never be paid above the bare minimum that ensures they can reproduce, history proved them wrong?

EPC — I prefer to say that, in 1848, Karl and Fred underestimated the power of the organized working class, especially with regards to reforms.

GE — Underestimated the power of the working class? That's a fairly provocative statement.

EPC — Perhaps, but they were relying on the evidence available to them.

GE — Let me repeat that just to make sure I heard you right. You're saying that, if anything, the Communist Manifesto underestimated, not overestimated, the power of the working class?

EPC — Exactly.

GE — Most critics have claimed the opposite. They say history proves Marx and Engels overestimated the power of the working class.

EPC — Well that's just plain stupid. They never foresaw that 90 percent of the population would become working class. Well, they did sort of predict it — they saw that the working class would become the majority — but from their perspective in 1848 they couldn't possibly have known that billions of people across the planet would become wage workers. Or that pretty much every conceivable occupation would become part of the working class. Or that there'd be as many women workers as men. Or that a shitload of what used to be management work would go to wage workers. How could they have figured all that out in 1848?

GE — If the working class has become even more powerful than Marx and Engels foresaw why has there been no revolution?

EPC — Because the vast majority of workers weren't interested in revolution — at least not in the sense of a violent overthrow of the existing order. They wanted reforms and that's what they achieved. The early Marx and Engels underestimated the power of the working class to achieve reforms.

GE — The power to achieve reforms?

EPC — Marx and Engels didn't see that workers would have the power to win reforms like public education, the 8-hour day, pensions, unemployment insurance, vacations, stat holidays, public healthcare, graduated income tax ... the list is very long. In 1848 Marx and Engels didn't think workers could even achieve decent wages, let alone all that other stuff.

GE — Without a revolution you mean? Marx and Engels thought it would take a revolution to get that stuff.

EPC — In 1848 they thought it would take a revolution. Later they saw more possibilities for reform.

GE — But you're saying something more than reforms have worked. You're saying workers don't like revolution. Why?

EPC — Because our experience shows most revolutions don't turn out well for ordinary people. Because any sane person prefers peaceful reform over violent revolution, if you can achieve the same end.

GE — That's a pretty big if.

EPC — I'd say the working-class experience so far is that reforms work a hell of a lot better than violent revolution. The places where we are the best off are precisely the places where unions and working-class political parties were most successful at getting reforms.

GE — But, recent history shows all of the reforms workers have won are at risk if we don't end the power of capitalists.

EPC — Absolutely right. Capitalists always want it all for themselves and try to get it. So long as capitalists have power, they will keep trying to screw us.

GE — But you think we can break their power without a revolution?

EPC — It will be the revolution when we end their power.

GE — So you are in favor of revolution?

EPC — Of course. But changing from one economic system to another takes a long time. Just look at the transition between capitalism and feudalism. How long did that take? Centuries. How many reforms were there over the few hundred years it took? Can you point to a time or place where there was feudalism one day and capitalism the next? No, because that's not the way real change happens.

GE — There was a lot of violence in the transition between feudalism and capitalism.

EPC — A lot. That's because the change from feudalism to capitalism was one form of minority rule taking over from another. All minority rule is violent. It has to be to achieve and maintain power. It's a small group using terror to rule a much larger group. The goal of the working class is to end minority rule, to replace capitalist title with economic democracy, to build a world based on human cooperation, democracy and equality.

GE — So, you're saying that because the working-class goal is economic democracy, violence won't be necessary?

EPC — Exactly. Violence on our part isn't necessary and certainly not desirable. Of course, there has been violence to repress us and will be more. But it will come from the ruling class protecting its minority rule. Capitalists control wealth, means of transportation and communications. They use the police and armed forces to protect their property rights, so anytime we resort to violence we get clobbered. In fact, violence suits the ruling class because they know they almost always win.

GE — So your objection is tactical, not a principle?

EPC — It's both. All the evidence shows that capitalism has a nearly limitless capacity for violence. It's a stupid tactic to fight them on a field where they have most of the advantages. With non-violent mass action it's our numbers that count. Non-violence is the tactic of the majority. But there's also an important principle. If you want to create a society where the majority really rules, where there is no more war and where we live in balance with nature, violence is our enemy. It can't be the source of our liberation. The society we want is against violence in principle.

GE — But just so I'm clear on this, you do acknowledge that there will be violent resistance to change?

EPC — Yes. There is and will be war. There's police violence. There's the violence of poverty. There's the masked violence of master-servant relations in corporate workplaces.

GE — How do you expect people to react to that?

EPC — Lots of people will react as they always have. They will be violent in return. I understand the reaction. I played hockey. But that reaction is the loser's reaction. It's defensive. We'll know we're getting close to winning when we can meet their violence with non-violence. After that it won't take long for people to understand that the ruling class's hold on society rests on violence. And once the vast majority of people understand that, the end is near for capitalism. The working-class uprising will be a general strike that becomes a lockout of the bosses. A permanent lockout. That will be the revolution.

GE — You're sure there will be an end to capitalism? Lots of people think capitalism is the best system in history or at least the best system possible today.

EPC — That's stupid. Where's the evidence for that?

GE — Supporters of capitalism say people live longer, have more freedoms, better housing, are more educated ...

EPC — It's cynical bullshit for capitalists to take credit for stuff they hate. People living longer, being better educated and having more freedoms are all the result of the organized working class fighting for reforms that capitalists opposed. Public health, public utilities, public education, the fight for voting rights for men with no property and then women's right to vote, civil rights, pensions, unemployment insurance — who fought for all these things? Us, the organized working class. It sure as hell wasn't capitalists. They fought against them all the way and continue to try to overturn the gains we've made.

GE — So you don't give capitalists credit for anything?

EPC — I give them credit for creating the working class.

GE — That's it?

EPC — They're good at waging war. And capitalism may be the best system at producing more. More and more. But often we don't need more. We need less, but better. More is killing us. It's spewing carbon into the atmosphere and warming up the planet. In some places it's giving us two or three cars per family and junk food, which is making us fat and also destroying the environment. More has been completely disconnected from what's good for us. It's really about more profit for capitalists.

GE — A lot of people like more.

EPC — They think they do, until they realize what it's doing to them and their families. Anybody with half a brain knows that over-consumption is bad and that capitalism is stupid. The best you can say about capitalism is that it gave us a lot of stuff and the most destructive wars in history, atomic bombs, obesity and global warming. We can do one hell of a lot better if we just come together and try.

GE — How would you say your views differ from what most people would consider typical Marxism?

EPC — Most people confuse Marxism with Leninism. Karl Marx would not have been a Leninist. He would have ridiculed the idea of a "vanguard" of revolutionaries who presume to lead the working class. That is not to say he rejected political parties with programs etc., but the idea of claiming a party could somehow permanently represent the interests of the class would have struck him as non-materialist, utopian at best and reactionary at worst.

GE — You're a longtime union activist. How is your version of Marxism connected to unions?

EPC — Marx spent the most intense political period of his life working to build the First International, which was a worldwide union federation. If he were alive today he'd still believe the best way to change the world is through building unions and other organizations of workers. Marx believed that positive change would come through a working-class revolution. He believed that working people had the power to challenge the strength of the minority who ruled the world. He believed the job of the communist was to educate workers to understand their power and their common interest in creating a better system, one that would end minority rule and be better for all.

GE — Are unions the only way to change the world?

EPC — Marx believed that workers need their own political party. That's more true today than ever. Marx wasn't a wage worker, but that didn't stop him from helping out. He believed in creating a world that offered every person the chance to lead a fulfilling life. He was convinced that minority class rule was responsible for stifling the creativity inherent in all of us. Throughout his life he campaigned for the expansion of democracy and human entitlement. If he were alive today, he would campaign for economic democracy. This includes the right of everyone to participate in economic decision-making, not just workers. Marx focused on wage workers, but he would see the value in getting the unemployed, the self-employed, stay-at-home parents, students and the retired involved in confronting capitalism.

GE — What would Marx think of current electoral politics.

EPC — He would be disgusted. Parties that call themselves Labor, Social Democratic and Socialist now rarely

14

criticize capitalism. Once in office, they insist that they have to govern for everyone, including capitalists and warmongers. They adopt domestic policies that widen disparities and support destructive military interventions abroad. Yes, Marx would likely look for ways to effect legislation that would improve the lives of common people. He'd be on the streets and in legislatures fighting against all forms of sexism, racism and homophobia. He'd be there with people defending immigrants' rights, with the housing advocates and the environmentalists. He would campaign for the rights of indigenous peoples to their lands, resources and ways of life. He'd see value in nationalism in the sense of belonging to a larger group, but he'd be a post-ethnic, internationalist nationalist, who fights for the rights of all nations to be respected.

GE — He'd be just like you?

EPC — You created me, so you would know.

GE — You said that capitalism is not compatible with environmental sustainability. Why do you say that?

EPC — Capitalism requires constant growth because it always needs more profit. More profit is the point of capitalism. If all you care about is making more stuff, capitalism is the best system ever. But what happens when the environment needs a smaller human footprint? When, at least in wealthier countries, we must learn to live with much less stuff? All the evidence shows capitalism is really lousy at dealing with declining markets. Every time the economy shrinks for a sustained period capitalism goes into a crisis. Banks crash, unemployment rises and wars are often necessary to get capitalism out of its crisis.

GE — But many people look to capitalism for solutions to our environmental problems.

EPC — That's like asking the fox to fix the henhouse. You can't be a serious environmentalist and support capitalism. A sustainable economy is incompatible with capitalism.

GE — Many environmentalists would disagree.

EPC — Sure, just like some so-called union leaders say they don't have any problem with capitalism. There's two possible explanations: One, they're just trying to work as best they can within the system, even if they hate it, because no alternative has been on offer that appeals to them. Or two, they're sellouts. Same goes for environmentalists who claim to support capitalism.

GE — So you write off most environmental groups?

EPC — Some existing environmental groups do good work to expose unsustainable industrial practices. But because they do not oppose capitalism they promote cap and trade, which leaves the adoption of sustainable practices to capitalist markets and that is ultimately a dead end. To be successful, environmental groups depend on funding. Because the rich have most of that, environmental groups avoid pointing to capitalism as the source of the problem. That will change as opposition to capitalism grows.

GE — You haven't even started writing the book and you've already pissed off three-quarters of the potential readers. No Marxists or mainstream environmentalists allowed.

EPC — I'm just being clear about my views. My biases. Let people know who I am and what I stand for. It's called honesty. I want everyone to read the book, but I don't want to fool anybody into thinking it's something other than what it is.

GE — Maybe we should get into how you plan to go about this — rewriting the Communist Manifesto in a way that makes it current, but also keeps it true to the essence of what Karl Marx and Friedrich Engels wrote in 1848?

EPC — First off, a lot has changed since the original Manifesto was written. In 1848 there were still feudal lords running most of the world. Slavery was still legal in most places. The First Opium War had ended a few years earlier during which Britain invaded China to force it to accept the importation of opium. The East India Company administered most of the Indian subcontinent. The carving up of Africa into European colonies had barely even begun. 1848 was more than a decade before Charles Darwin published *On The Origin of Species*. The vast majority of people everywhere worked on the land. Racism was just about to become a dominant ideology. The New Manifesto has to reflect all that's happened since 1848.

GE — Given how old it is, do you think the original Communist Manifesto is still relevant?

EPC — It's one of the most influential pamphlets ever written. It inspired workers' movements, unions and political parties all over the world. To this day the Manifesto is probably the best easy-to-read criticism of capitalism. To understand the past 165 years of opposition to capitalism, you have to read it. Anybody who decides there's something wrong with capitalism owes it to herself to read it. Every person who has ever wondered why going to work feels so shitty owes it to himself to read it. Everybody who comes to believe a better system is possible simply must take a look at what a 30-year-old Karl Marx and 28-year-old Freddy Engels wrote in 1848. Not bad for two young German intellectuals who never had a working-class job in their entire lives.

GE — If it's so good, why bother updating it?

EPC — Exactly what I thought at first. How can the Communist Manifesto be "improved" anymore than Picasso's painting Guernica or Diego Rivera's mural in the Mexican national palace be "updated" or in any way made better? But then it occurred to me that today's Pakistani artists should try to capture the horror of U.S. drone missile attacks on village wedding parties just like Picasso exposed the inhumanity of German bombs falling on the small Basque city. And Rivera's work did inspire others to tell the story of their communities on walls around the world.

GE — Picasso's picture, Rivera's mural and the Communist Manifesto were all calls to action. The creators wanted to change the world.

EPC — And so do I.

GE — How do you want to change the world?

EPC — Well, as I wrote in the *Great Multicultural North*, I believe in a post-ethnic, internationalist nationalism and economic democracy. I want a world where one person, one vote rules all social aspects of our lives. I want to get rid of capitalism's one dollar, one vote. I believe capitalism is neither democratic nor compatible with environmental sustainability. I think all that is in the tradition of the Communist Manifesto.

GE — What parts of the old Manifesto need to be changed to make it current? And what needs to be added?

EPC — Like I said, a lot has happened in 165 years, the working class has had a lot of experience. This needs to be reflected. There's stuff to get rid of, but you can't throw the political baby out with the historical bathwater. Things must be added. Environmentalism is the big one. What would Karl and Freddy have said about that, if they had the benefit of the last 165 years of science and working-class experience?

GE — There's a lot to think about. Maybe you should get at it.

EPC — Since when are you my boss?

GE — You only exist when I let you.

EPC — Said the worker to the capitalist.

GE — And the capitalist to the worker. Which one is right?

EPC — Both are right from their points of view.

GE — How can both be right?

EPC — They're talking about different things. The worker is saying that under a different system she wouldn't need the capitalist. The capitalist is saying capitalism gives him the power to determine whether the worker has a job or not.

GE — Please stop talking and start writing.

EPC — Fine, okay. We'll talk again when I'm done.

Glossary

One way the system controls us is by making important words – pretty much any necessary to truly explain capitalism – seem strange, almost taboo. To break free we must use and understand language that serves our interests. For example, we should always use the term working class, not middle class, to refer to wage workerss. Below I have defined a few of the essentials.— Ernie

Capital: Private title to means of livelihood – land, resources, technologies, machinery, equipment, supplies and stocks of commodities – and to the profits, rents and interest generated by social labour. It appears as money and is security for most credit. The owners of it get special privileges over the rest of us, sort of like those that flowed from feudalism's concept of the divine right of kings.

Capitalism: A system of minority privilege and class rule based on the private ownership of means of livelihood. The right of capitalists to buy and sell means of livelihood without regard to the workers and communities that depend on them. Under capitalism those with the most capital are entitled to the most goods and services as well as the most say in directing means of livelihood and social labour.

Capitalist class: People whose income largely comes from owning capital. As little as 0.01 per cent – major shareholders and top corporate executives – effectively control most capital. The equivalent to "nobilty" under feudalism. Think of billionionaires as being kings and lesser capitalists as dukes, barons etc. They often go on about the virtues of individual enterprise, all the while making their profits from the social labor of workers.

Capitalist title: Ownership of means of livelihood based on wealth. Before capitalism, kings or lords claimed title to most property. For common people, rights to lands, resources, buildings, equipment were based on possession and custom. Under capitalism, legally enforced documents called title deeds replaced customary usage as the source of property rights. As feudalism turned into capitalism, people lost customary rights. What had been commonly held village lands were fenced and declared private property. Familes who had for generations lived on the land, grown food, gathered wood in forests and grazed animals were driven from their cottages. In one way or another lawyers, merchants, aristocrats and wealthier freeholders were able to produce title deeds that "proved" their private ownership.

Economic democracy: Communities replace corporations as the owners of social means of livelihood. In place of the "one dollar, one vote" of capitalism, everyone will be entitled to a voice and equal vote in economic decisions. Master-servant relations are replaced by the right of workers in all occupations to democratically direct their social labour time. Real, instead of pretend, government for the people by the people.

Enclosures: The fencing and privatization of common lands that drove away families who had for generations lived on the land, grown food and grazed animals.

Master-servant relations: The dictatorship of the boss. The laws and rules that govern workplaces, which mean workers must do as employers say or be fired. Unions give workers some extra rights, which is the reason most bosses hate unions.

Social labour: Work that requires the cooperation of numerous workers to be completed. Most goods and services now require social labour to be conceived, processed, produced, transported and exchanged. Despite the collective nature of this work, capitalists claim ownership of the product and demand that social labour be directed in their private interests.

Working class: People who depend on income from their labour. Wage and salary workers, people engaged in social labour, are the vast majority of the working class in more prosperous countries. The self-employed — farmers, shopkeepers, doctors, lawyers etc. — are ten per cent or so of populations in the richest parts of the world. They, along with some professionals and managers, are the real middle class. Almost everyone who depends on income from their labour, not on capital, is part of the working class. This includes students, pensioners, full-time parents and those dependent on social assistance. Because we do almost everything useful in the economy we have the power to change the world.

The New Commune-ist Manifesto

Introduction

Capitalism is a system that entitles major shareholders and top corporate executives — less than one percent of populations — to direct means of livelihood in their private interests. Driven by competition to maximize profits, capitalists relentlessly expand production, while cutting employment and wages. Booms are followed by busts. Environmental costs are externalized and ignored. Disparities widen and the system relies more on propaganda, repression and war.

But, as capitalism has become increasingly incompatible with human wellbeing, opposition to the system has withered away. In the 19th and 20th centuries, the Communist Manifesto's ideas and platform inspired movements for workers' rights and democracy, for public education, universal health care, pensions and unemployment insurance, against racism, and for national liberation and women's rights. Twentieth century working-class gains that made life under capitalism more tolerable could have inspired movements for fundamental change. Unfortunately the alternative had come to be seen as Communist Party rule as practised in the Soviet Union. One-party dictatorship, repression and relative poverty was not an inspiring alternative. Capitalism was allowed to identify with democracy.

Today, in the name of democracy, capitalists justify their minority rule, invade other countries, destroy cities, kill thousands and displace millions. At home, corporate oligarchs use their wealth to manipulate political power, to undermine social programs, weaken unions and lower real wages. When people anywhere rally in support of real democracy, capitalists and their sycophants in government, academia, the media and political parties label them populist troublemakers, anarchists or communists. To impose their agendas, capitalists turn to capital strikes, tear gas and riot police.

Their disregard for human wellbeing is obvious in the system's failure to act to reverse climate change. Faced with overwhelming evidence that carbon emissions are leading to environmental catastrophe, capitalists use their wealth to deny the problem and weaken environmental legislation. They do so because their profits, their wealth and power are tied to the burning of fossil fuels.

Two important points need to be made:

First, capitalist entitlement is the most serious threat facing humankind. Second, the working class — the overwhelming majority that relies on its labor, not on capitalist entitlement, for its livelihood — now clearly has the capacity to build economic democracy.

Expanding democracy is critical to saving our planet and making a better life for every person in the world. Democracy does not mean arbitrary power for a few. It means the right of everyone to an equal claim to ownership of their communities' social means of livelihood and an equal right to participate in economic decisions. It means providing everyone on our planet with an equal right to have his or her needs met. It means the right of people in all occupations to participate as equals in directing their social labor time.

The old communism is dead. Long live the new communism! The new communism does not mean centralized state ownership and top-down party rule. It means commune-ism. A commune is a local district, its land, people and the way they make social decisions. A commune could be as small as a village or as large as a major city. Commune-ism means direction of resources and social labor from the bottom up. Today in a world of global markets and nation states, that means ownership by local communities, towns, cities, provinces/states, regions, national governments and by democratic, transparent international institutions.

The New Commune-ist Manifesto has been published so that people around the world who see the need for real, economic democracy — the essence of communism — can read, discuss, debate and come together to clarify views and aims so that our movement, the new commune-ism, can grow.

We write in English but look forward to versions in many languages.

I — Capitalists and Workers

1. Minority rule

Class struggle has dominated human history since agriculture made it practical for people to regularly produce more than they needed to survive. Violent armed minorities found they could appropriate goods produced by others and force the majority to work on their behalf. Armed gangs simply took, or laid claim to lands, waterways, natural resources and human activity. Conqueror and conquered, free person and slave, patrician and plebian, lord and serf, guild master and journeyman stood in constant opposition to each other, carried on a constant, sometimes hidden, sometimes open fight. Oppressors and the oppressed carried on disputes that led eventually either to a reconstitution of society or to the common ruin of the contending classes.

The origins of minority rule are theft and its first cousin warfare. For more than three thousand years religion and philosophy have insisted that class privilege is the natural, God-given, way of the world. Contrary opinions and thoughts have been declared sinful and criminal, punished by beatings and torture, imprisonment and death. To give ruling minorities more power, the natural functions associated with sexuality and reproduction were deemed shameful unless strictly regulated. What women should and cannot do have been narrowly defined to make it appear that all men share in ruling-class privilege.

Before capitalism, ruling minorities had established complicated social arrangements, with multiple ranks, almost always originating from male warrior cultures that overthrew older egalitarian female-centered social relations. Early class societies in China, India, Egypt, Peru, Mexico, Greece and Rome all had people who counted most (the usually male ruling class), people who counted less but were still important (knights and religious leaders for example), people who counted for almost nothing (women, plebeians and peasants) and people who were nothing more than the property of others (slaves).

These minority-ruled societies invented writing, so they could keep records of what they owned and what others owed them. They wrote the earliest histories. We have no stories written by the many people across the planet who lived in egalitarian societies.

In medieval Europe, feudalism was the traditional form of minority rule. After the collapse of the Roman Empire, gangs of armed men looted and plundered places where people relied on subsistence farming and associated handicrafts. Sometimes these gangs hung around, claiming ownership of lands by right of inheritance from past or mythical rulers. They then demanded payments for protection against other gangs. Farmers were forced to choose between paying a portion of their crop and providing labor services, or being victimized by sword and pillage. Over time the most powerful of these gang leaders established courts and became kings. They made leaders of smaller gangs their vassals and claimed their earthly power was God-given.

In feudal times, 80 or 90 percent of most populations lived on the land, as they had for millennia, relying on local resources, growing much of their families' food and working at traditional handicrafts. Production for exchange had its own customary rules. Mostly for local markets, it was organized by closed guilds dominated by wealthier shop owners in each trade who typically spent at least some time working at their own crafts. Guilds decided who could enter trades, regulated quality and set prices.

2. Early capitalism

Mercantile capitalism emerged in northern Italy, the Netherlands, and then in England. At first merchants would buy finished products, often from the guilds who made the goods, and then sold these into markets where the prices were higher.

This, of course, gave the biggest profits to the merchants who knew best where to buy low and sell high. But after a while some merchants got the idea that they could make even more profit by what came to be called the putting-out system. This was a way to get around guild regulations and undercut the usual prices. Merchants provided artisans — spinners, weavers, button-makers, etc. who worked outside guild jurisdiction, often in the countryside — with materials on credit, and then purchased the finished products, selling these wherever they could get the highest prices. The putting-out system weakened the guilds and gave the new "capitalists" wealth and political influence. Their fortunes and power were further enhanced by advancing seafaring technology. Fifteenth-century European ships sailed around Africa to India, Indonesia and China, then "discovered" the Americas. By the 16th century, private fortunes were being made in plunder, piracy and trade in gold, silver, spices, ivory, fish, furs and timber. By the 17th century more great capitalist fortunes were made in tobacco, sugar, cotton and coffee plantations. Also profitable was transporting and selling slaves from Africa who did much of the work.

As capitalist wealth grew, merchants, lawyers, aristocrats and freeholders used their political influence to further enclose commons. Land that had been held in common by villagers was fenced and declared private property. This had begun in the 16th century in England when landowners began to raise sheep on land that had for centuries been used by commoners. More and more people who had had customary rights to village lands for subsistence were driven away by court order and militias working in the interests of lords and capitalists (one was often the other).

As desperate people fled to urban centers, towns and cities grew while wages fell. With cheaper labor and growing demand, the putting-out system mostly disappeared. Capitalists decided that assembling workers in factories and assigning most of them simple repetitive tasks, which could be closely supervised, would increase profits. Men, women and children came to be employed in factories for 16 and 18 hours a day for wages that were often not enough for the food needed to survive. The less fortunate were worked to death in workhouses, or indentured to plantation owners and transported abroad. (For plantation owners, forced labor from the home countries turned out to be insecure. Those who escaped could easily blend in among free settlers. Africans were easier to identify as escaped slaves.)

Supporters of the system like to claim that capitalism freed people from feudal obligations and duties. It did, if freedom means suffering and death. Alongside the thousands of villagers dispossessed by enclosures and victimized by the early factory system, millions of Africans died at the hands of slavers and plantation overseers. In the New World, millions of indigenous people lost their lives in the European pursuit of gold, silver and land. Asians lost control of their countries to foreign invasion.

If freedom means power over others, capitalists were freed. By the 16th century, the bourgeoisie — guild masters, lawyers, bankers, merchants — were the ruling classes of major cities. By the end of the 17th century, capitalist wealth was coming to challenge hereditary feudal entitlements even in royal courts. Over time, the rise of the urban bourgeoisie meant that republics replaced monarchies, but governments continued to be directed by and in the interests of a minority.

For the mass of people early capitalism meant the loss of customary rights, starvation, or poorly-paid and mind-numbing labor. Few had any real choice. Enclosures had denied rural artisans the right to land for subsistence. The rising productivity of factory labor reduced prices, making it impractical for independent artisans to support their families or themselves. As more people lost the means to support themselves, poverty drove them to seek wage work. Desperation and competition among workers drove wage rates down further. Those who did not succeed in getting wage work were left to live in dispiriting poverty, to die unknown.

Division of labor in the factory system simplified tasks to the point that many could be performed by machines. The age of steam engines and assembly lines had begun. Hundreds and sometimes thousands of workers were brought together in factories, dramatically increasing the quantity and quality of goods that could be produced by a given amount of labor, and increasing the profits of capital.

As machine industry expanded, villages became towns. Migration severed customary human connections with nature, a process that has continued around the world to this day, to the detriment of the planet. By 1848 half the English population had come to live in cities, where wealth was concentrated in fewer hands and jobs could be found in factories.

Before capitalism, ruling-class privilege, customs, laws and modes of livelihood were viewed as unchanging and unchangeable. Capitalism revolutionized modes of production, industrial techniques, transportation, methods of building, the layout of cities, communications and the technologies of warfare. Under capitalism, where money is the sole standard of value and wealth is the only source of entitlement, nearly everything changes — except rule on behalf of capitalists.

In England capitalism had made most rural and urban handicraft production obsolete by 1848. Factory production in Britain, Europe and North America steadily expanded. Coal-fired steam engines revolutionized transportation. Railways, telegraph lines and steam-powered freighters transformed the planet into a single market. Although goods, people and armies could be moved nearly everywhere, major capitalist powers were competing to divide Asia, Africa and South America into colonies and spheres of influence. International markets were divided among rival imperial blocs.

While slavery had been abolished in most countries, factory, mine, forest and service workers even in the wealthiest countries lived in poverty. So did most small farmers. Capitalism spread to the colonies and neo-colonies. Dispossessed rural populations in India, China and elsewhere lost access to lands for subsistence. Competition with European machine industry meant that peasants could no longer survive in the off-seasons on income earned from spinning and weaving. Millions died in recurring famines. In Mexico, Central and South America, in nominally independent countries dominated by U.S. and European capital, debt peonage in sugar, coffee, cotton, sisal and rubber plantations was not much of an improvement over slavery.

3. Twentieth century capitalism

By the twentieth century, corporate enterprises were absorbing suppliers, marketing networks and former competitors within countries and across borders. Corporate growth, mergers and acquisitions diluted the ownership stake of founding families. Capital, no longer tied to particular corporations, was freed to move in pursuit of the highest profits, from one enterprise to others, from industry to industry and from country to country. Speculation, not enterprise, became the defining activity of capitalists. Financial institutions too big to fail came to play an increasingly central role in the allocation of capital.

But imperial protectionism and fascism in the first half of the twentieth century delayed the unrestricted mobility of capital, which later would come to be known as globalization. Inter-imperialist rivalry led to the European war of 1914-18. Aggressively emerging imperial Germany, allied with the declining Austro-Hungarian and Ottoman empires, challenged British, French and Dutch global domination. Tens of millions died.

Victory was claimed by the U.K. and France, which at the beginning of the war had been allied with Czarist Russia, as well as with Italy and Japan. In 1917 the U.S. also entered the war on their side, but the war was actually brought to an end by mass uprisings. In Russia troops refused to obey orders to go to the front; workers took charge of factories and railways, and the country withdrew from the war. In 1918 German sailors refused to obey orders; they set up councils to take charge of ships; workers in shipyards and munitions industries set up councils to run their workplaces. A paralyzed imperial Germany sued for peace. A war that had horrified and exhausted European populations ended. But the U.K., France, USA and Canada sent troops to overthrow Bolshevik rule. They failed. Troops transported to the Soviet Union mutinied, refusing to obey orders. Back home, workers refused to load munitions.

During the war, the Allies proclaimed their commitment to the self-determination of nations. After the war, the Allies claimed possession of German colonies. Arab nations, formerly part of the Ottoman Empire, were divided up as protectorates of France and Britain. Monarchies dependent on imperial interests were imposed on the people. The war had made it clear that oil would be the critical resource for the rest of the century.

In Germany nationalists bitterly resented the loss of territory and the reparations the country had to pay in what had been an inter-imperialist war. Capitalists in Italy and Japan resented not being awarded additional colonies. Italy turned to fascism in the early 1920s. Japan and Germany would follow a decade later.

Fascism was anti-democratic and rejected the principle that law should apply equally. Fascists held that women should be restricted to childrearing and housework. They accepted that ruling-class power and privilege rested on violent repression, and looked to war to expand imperial rule. Of course all imperialist powers relied on militarism and claims of racial superiority. But fascism made warfare, the occupation of foreign lands and racism the foundations of their social order.

In Italy support for fascism came from capitalists who were faced with factory occupations, from major landowners and from the Catholic hierarchy. Mussolini aimed to transform the Mediterranean into an Italian sea through conquests in north Africa and south-eastern Europe. In Japan support for fascism came from the officer corps and monopoly capitalists who were tied to the imperial court. Japanese militarists set out to conquer and transform the countries of continental Asia into Japanese colonies.

In Germany support for the Nazis came from the officer corps, veterans and the owners of industrial cartels. Nazis held that Germany had been made to unfairly pay the price of an inter-imperialist war. They proclaimed their intention to exterminate Jews, inferior races, the physically and mentally abnormal, homosexuals, communists, socialists, independent unionists and cosmopolitan intellectuals. They proposed building a Third Reich, a new German empire in eastern Europe that would transform Slavic lands into living space for German colonists.

In the second inter-imperialist war a total of nearly 25 million soldiers died. German armies suffered their heaviest casualties in fighting the Soviet Union. Japan suffered its heaviest casualties fighting Nationalist and Communist armies in China. In Germany three million civilians lost their lives, a half million were Jews. Five million civilians were killed in Poland, half of whom were Jews. More than 12 million Soviet civilians died, close to a quarter were Jews. Twenty million civilians lost their lives in China.

At the Bretton Woods resort in New Hampshire in 1944 allied governments agreed to regulate exchange rates, capital flows and interest rates. Tariffs were to be kept low enough to revive international trade, but high enough to encourage domestic production for domestic markets. After the war, capitalist governments adopted Keynesian policies and launched the Cold

War against Communism. Labor laws were changed to make it easier for unions to organize and to engage in collective bargaining. Governments provided public pensions, family allowances, unemployment insurance, as well as expanding access to education and healthcare. Military spending was kept high. Infrastructure spending on highways, communications systems and on electricity development and distribution was justified as required to protect against Communist attacks. In the most prosperous countries real wages grew steadily. Official unemployment rates were low. Growing working-class income led to steady increases in sales of automobiles and suburban houses.

In former colonies and semi-colonies, in China, India, Indonesia, the Middle East and much of Latin America, mass movements were gaining national sovereignty. In countries like India, where Communists had not taken power, Keynesian policies were the rule. Governments acted to improve education, healthcare, social infrastructure, and to lay the foundations for industrial production and expanding international trade. But most enterprises remained in the hands of private capital. Rural areas continued to be impoverished. Aboriginal people and peasants lost lands to capitalist development. Millions of the dispossessed fled to cities.

As more countries gained formal independence, a new corporate imperialism emerged. In the Middle East monarchies that had been imposed by Britain and France were brought to an end. The military coups responsible claimed to represent common people, but they either accommodated to transnational corporate power or were overthrown. In the 1950s a monarchist coup in Iran, organized by the U.S. embassy and oil interests, overthrew a democratically elected government. In Guatemala U.S. interests overthrew a popular government to reverse land reform. In Vietnam Ho Chi Minh's Communist forces defeated the French.

To counter the success of anti-colonial movements the U.S. set up a puppet government in South Vietnam and launched a massive but ultimately unsuccessful military assault that lasted almost two decades. U.S. corporate interests also supported and helped organize military coups in Brazil, Chile, Argentina, Paraguay, Uruguay, Haiti and other countries. In Africa armed forces from the U.S., France, Britain, Portugal and white South Africa intervened to protect and advance the interests of multinational mining and petroleum corporations.

Fewer and fewer giant corporations, based mostly in the U.S., but also from Britain, Europe, Japan and Canada dominated global markets. Relying on control of resources, intellectual property rights, transportation and distribution networks, they manipulated markets and set prices. They spent hundreds of millions annually on advertising to effectively exclude smaller enterprises from markets. In the early 1970s, U.S. President Richard Nixon terminated the Bretton Woods Agreement. Governments no longer intervened to direct currency levels or interest rates. Capital was freed to move nearly anywhere in pursuit of higher profits. Meanwhile, the normalization of U.S. relations with China, also under Nixon, made it practical for the Communist Party leadership to turn to capitalist development. China would be transformed into the hub of offshore corporate manufacturing.

By the late 1960s and early 1970s growing numbers were coming to see that corporate development and runaway consumerism were threatening the natural environment. Industrial air pollution was leading directly to urban health issues. Scientists were pointing out that petroleum-based chemical pesticides and fertilizers were destroying soil life, polluting streams, lakes and the ocean, as well as leading to troubling health issues among agricultural workers, farmers and consumers.

By the late 1970s scientists, environmentalists, writers and lovers of nature around the world were reporting that carbon dioxide emissions from the burning of fossil fuels were raising atmospheric temperatures and acidifying oceans. (Carbon dioxide joined with water forms carbonic acid, which reacts with the calcium in the shells of crustaceans, undermining coral reefs and threatening the survival of microorganisms that are the base of the ocean food chain.) Scientists predicted that rising temperatures would radically alter weather patterns, make severe storms more common and melt polar ice caps. Rising sea levels would flood areas inhabited by much of the human population.

4. Social labour replaces the individual in the market

In 1848, when the Communist Manifesto was published, wage workers were not a majority anywhere, not even in England. Most people were still small holders, cottagers, sharecroppers, in-house servants, artisans, shopkeepers, self-employed professionals or precariously employed, such as artists, actors and musicians. Servants and shop assistants were part of the working class, but were in patron-client relations and most of their pay was in clothing, food and lodging. Today as much as 90 percent of the population in many countries work for wages, with others, in cooperative, coordinated, social labor. But economies are directed to provide profit for major shareholders and top corporate executives, at most one or two percent of populations.

The old Manifesto focused on industrial workers. It did not predict the proletarianization of women or of most salaried employment. Beginning in the 1830s legislation in Britain prohibited the employment of children in factories and mines and restricted the employment of women. By banning the exploitation of the most vulnerable these reforms were beneficial. However, these laws also denied women equal employment rights. Although women continued to be employed in industry, in textile and clothing factories, most women were employed in domestic service, as maids, cooks, governesses and companions. Then, by the end of the 19th century, women were employed as sales clerks, telephone operators and typists. During the European war of 1914-18, the conscription and slaughter of millions of men led to rapid growth in employment of women in war industries. After the First World War and then again after the war of 1939-45 many women lost their jobs to returned soldiers.

Still, women in growing numbers were employed in low paying jobs in textiles, food processing, retail and services. The increase in the number of women working for wages was made practical by corporate food processing and the mechanization of housework. Contrary to prejudices of the time, most women were not working for pin money. Most women worked because they had to. In the days before industrial unions, wages paid to men working in factories were not enough to support a family. Women were just as likely as men to join unions. In the first three decades of the 20th century women participated in and led militant strikes in textiles, light manufacturing and telephone companies, workplaces where women were often the majority. In spite of capitalist exploitation, many women saw employment as liberating. Getting their own pay cheques freed women from financial dependence on fathers, husbands or brothers.

Most salaried employees before the 20th century were men in client-patron relations with their employers. Compared to wage workers, their employment was more secure, they were paid more, often had pensions and could expect to rise through the ranks. Many identified with top management and with minority entitlement.

Salaried work was proletarianized as capital was centralized in larger corporations and governments became providers of social services. Corporations relentlessly expanded, merging with and acquiring competitors. As corporations became larger, chains of command became longer and broader and more salaried employees were required.

Government salaried employment also expanded substantially, taking on responsibility for education, pensions, employment insurance, welfare benefits, healthcare, as well as for internal and external security.

Larger, layered corporate and government offices came to rely more on machines — telephones, typewriters, dictaphones, copiers, calculators and then computers. Factory-like divisions of labor followed. Most of the lower-paid jobs came to be done by women. Men continued to hold the higher-paid positions.

Computers made it practical to centralize more decision-making. Fewer middle and lower-level managers were required. Salaried, university-educated technical and professional specialists, like manufacturing workers, faced the loss of employment to machine technology and to lower-paid workers in other parts of the world. The capitalist disregard for the interests of salaried workers was accompanied by concerted campaigns against "bureaucracies." Corporate bosses and the politicians they financed were particularly aggressive in denouncing workers employed by government as unacceptable burdens on taxpayers.

Factory work has declined relative to other forms of wage labor in the most prosperous countries. But the portion of the population who rely on wage work has grown everywhere. The laboring class has become more diverse. It now includes people who operate machines in manufacturing, transportation and services. It includes people engaged in the administration of private industry and social services. It includes people who have learned their skills on the job, as well as the technically and professionally certified.

In Europe, Japan, North America and other countries, 90 percent of people now depend on income from their labor. Ten percent remain self employed: shopkeepers, self-employed professionals, equipment owner-operators and farmers. For most of the self-employed, capital is not a source of income; it is a burden: rent that must be paid to landowners, or interest that must be paid to banks. Some of the self-employed, like a few of the highest paid wage and salary workers, may over time become capitalists in their own right by investing in real estate or the stock market. But most will remain dependent on income from their labor.

In the poorest countries, former colonies or semi-colonies, dominated by transnational agriculture, timber, or mining corporations, majorities may continue to be small landholders, share croppers, or petty street traders. But even in these countries, rapidly growing numbers are becoming dependent on social labor.

Globally, wage and salary workers now do everything necessary for human wellbeing. Arrayed against the working class are the real beneficiaries of capitalism, the plutocrats, the one percent, or, to be more precise, the 0.01 percent. Ultra High Net Worth Individuals — major shareholders and top corporate executives — today have annual incomes of more than $5 million a year and assets of more than $50 million. They may reside in the U.S., China, the E.U., Russia, Brazil, but their community is transnational. Everywhere capitalism gives them the right to direct economies in their narrow class interests.

Who can reasonably dispute the old Manifesto's prediction that capitalism would divide people into an overwhelming majority who live by selling their labor power and a miniscule minority of incredibly wealthy capitalists?

5. Working-class gains

Although capitalism now faces little explicit opposition, working people have been successfully challenging capitalist entitlement for more than 200 years. At the beginning of the 19th century, when participation in a union was a crime punishable by transportation abroad, enslavement or death, English ship crews struck the masts and refused to work. In the 1820s, after numerous strikes, imprisonments and hangings, laws defining unions as criminal conspiracies began to be repealed. Miners, weavers, textile workers and skilled tradesmen organized for collective bargaining. Workers formed associations such as the Chartists in Britain to campaign for free assembly, freedom of association, freedom of speech and the right to vote. In the late 19th century mass women's movements, supported by unions, campaigned for the vote and equal rights for women. At the beginning of the 20th century most property qualifications were removed and working-class men gained the right to vote. Women in many countries soon won the same right.

By the middle of the century the growth of industrial unions meant that more than half of wage workers in the richest countries were engaged in collective bargaining, denying capital the right to unilaterally set the terms and conditions of employment. Labor-supported political parties were winning elections and forming coalitions. Laws were changed to make it easier for unions to organize and engage in collective bargaining. Governments followed Keynesian policies providing pensions, unemployment insurance, family allowances and increasing access to post-secondary education.

From the end of the 1939-45 war to the 1970s, real wages grew steadily in much of the dominant capitalist world. Working people were able to purchase goods and services that were not even available to the high aristocracy in earlier centuries. (The Manifesto predicted that capitalism would expand production and consumption to levels that could not have been imagined in pre-capitalist time.) Capitalism got the credit, but most of these gains can be attributed to collective bargaining by trade unions and to social reforms won by labor-supported political parties. And yes, there was also an element of the ruling class that wanted to prove its system was better for workers than the "socialist" states.

In the same period anti-colonial movements, relying on the mass support of workers and peasants, were bringing direct imperial rule to an end. Civil rights movements were making institutional racism illegal. Women were joining and forming unions. In workplaces, communities and schools women were mobilizing against restrictions in employment, against discriminatory wage rates, for an end to laws that denied women financial equality, and to establish the right of women to control their bodies.

Meanwhile, communism and opposition to capitalism had come to be identified with the USSR. By the 1960s the Soviet Communist Party dictatorship was widely seen as authoritarian and repressive. The Soviet Union was not overtaking capitalism; it was falling behind in the quantity and quality of available consumer goods. In the dominant capitalist countries support for communism and organized working-class opposition to capitalism largely disappeared.

6. Capitalist reaction

By the 1970s a capitalist reaction against welfare state policies was gaining momentum. The super-rich were appalled by expanding social entitlements, collective bargaining gains and growing demands for equal rights by racialized minorities, immigrants and women. They complained that the capitalist share of total income had become unacceptably low. They claimed to be under-appreciated and that the space for individual enterprise was steadily shrinking. The rich funded a populist movement supposedly to defend individual entrreprise. But it was capitalism, not social programs, that undermined the individual in the market. Markets everywhere had come to be dominated by giant multinational corporations, the largest of which had more revenues than most governments. Like authoritarian governments, corporate decisions were made by top-down hierarchic chains of command.

The power of corporations over markets and over social labor was not a problem for the super-rich. Corporations were responsible not to the masses but to major shareholders and top corporate executives. New conservatives were making it clear that they would not tolerate opposition to capitalist entitlement. They aggressively called for increased internal repression and promoted militarism and war abroad.

Declining economic growth, accompanied by rising inflation in the 1970s, provided neo-conservatives with a persuasive argument against Keynesian welfare state policies. For the super-rich this was an opportunity to return to the idealized free market policies of the late nineteenth century. Their family foundations and the corporations they controlled poured millions into right-wing think tanks, lobbied the media and educational institutions and generously funded politicians who advocated laws that undermined unions, eliminated social programs and reduced government regulation of corporations.

In 1979 Margaret Thatcher was elected prime minister in Britain. In 1980 Ronald Reagan was elected president of the USA. Once in office these neo-conservatives cut taxes paid by top income earners and corporations. They used the government deficits that followed to justify cuts to spending on social programs. Labor laws were changed to make union organizing and collective bargaining more difficult. Employers were given the legal right to openly interfere in union organizing. The right of unions to contribute to political parties was restricted. Corporations were freed from government regulations.

Neo-conservatives claimed that Keynesian demand-side policies (full employment, progressive taxation, generous social programs, etc.), which had been introduced decades earlier to save capitalism, had led to inflation and declining investment. They promised to focus on the supply-side — to put more money in the hands of the rich. This they insisted would lead to higher rates of investment and sustained economic growth. By 2000, the top one percent of income earners in the U.S. and U.K. had doubled their share of national income to 20 percent. But the rate of investment in those countries actually declined. When they did invest, corporations did so abroad where labor was cheaper. In the countries that initiated neo-conservative policies growth slowed and unemployment became persistently higher.

This should not have been a surprise. As capital increased its share of income the proportion going to everyone else declined. Consumer income stagnated and fell; real wages declined; markets shrank. So did domestic investment. With more investment dollars chasing fewer investment opportunities share prices rose. Stock market booms were followed by economic crashes. The first in October 1987 was viewed as no more than a market correction. In 2000 the high-tech bubble burst: Companies whose share value was measured in the billions disappeared. In 2007-09 the collapse of the sub-prime mortgage market vaporized some 15 to 30 trillion dollars in financial assets. Governments responded by providing trillions in bailout funds to financial institutions that had caused the crash. Most of these survived, some thrived. Corporations, facing more steeply declining markets and lower profits, responded by discharging workers, cutting wages and moving ever more jobs to places with lower wage rates. The continuing slump was made worse by the fact that most governments had come to accept neo-conservative policies, now called "neo-liberalism" or "the Washington consensus".

Accepting the dogma that economic growth requires increased title deeds, funds in the hands of investors, governments cut taxes paid by corporations and the rich. They freeze and cut social entitlements and public employment. The result: Already stagnant markets decline; investors acting in their private interests see even less reason to invest in real means of livelihood.

Although a third of humankind remains mired in poverty, current laissez faire capitalism has been accompanied by significant economic growth in parts of China, India, the Middle East and Latin America. In part this is a result of earlier state-sponsored construction of railways, highways, ports and communication facilities. In part it is a consequence of the flight of capital from

43

higher wage places. From a working-class perspective, reducing poverty and more equitably distributing employment opportunities is beneficial. But basing growth on the cheapening of labor undermines the purchasing capacity of majorities who depend on income from labor. This is unsustainable even from a capitalist perspective. As corporate profits rise, markets for consumer goods decline. Booms are followed by busts.

The capitalist reaction did make corporate oligarchs richer. It also made it clear that liberal ideologues were wrong to claim that Keynesian policies had transformed capitalism into something more accurately called market democracy. Keynesian policies did for a time dampen the short-sighted competitive greed of unrestrained capitalism. But Keynesianism deliberately left control of most means of livelihood in the hands of private capital. So long as their system seemed threatened by mass opposition, communism and unions, capitalists were prepared to make compromises. Once they became convinced that capitalism faced no organized challenge, capitalists abandoned Keynesian compromises. To reassert the primacy of capitalist interests, all they had to do was spend small portions of the socially-produced surpluses they controlled to finance right-wing think tanks, influence the media, as well as fund and lobby political parties.

Liberal theorists, who held that capitalism had morphed into market democracy, claimed that it had become a system of relatively equal contending elites who democratically competed for political and social influence. But, once capitalists acted to assert their primacy, elites in politics, government, the media, academia, religions, the military, the professions and unions either towed the company line or were pushed aside. The notion of contending elites was an illusion. Because capitalists control means of livelihood, direct social wealth, and own social surpluses, they have the power to run the system in their interests. Calling capitalism market democracy is deliberately deceptive. Democratic rights have advanced under capitalism, but over the objection of capitalists. Capitalist rights are property rights, not human rights. In corporate governance, those with the most shares get the most votes. Neither employees nor people in the communities where they operate have a voice or vote in decisions. Corporate bureaucracies are even more hierarchical and authoritarian than most states.

Economic decisions under capitalism are made not by the invisible hand of market forces for the benefit of all, but by major shareholders and top corporate executives in the interests of the one percent or 0.01 percent. What are called market forces are no more than the sum of decisions made by capitalists in their own interests.

7. Consequences of capitalism

Capitalists as individuals may or may not be obsessively greedy, but the system of competitive capitalist entitlement compels them to maximize profits. Capital with higher returns gains value; capital with lower returns loses value. Enterprises losing relative value are threatened by takeover, or being broken up and sold off in pieces, or being forced into bankruptcy. Competition to maximize profits explains why capitalist enterprises cut employment and wages with little or no regard for the effect on working people. It explains why corporations and the wealthy campaign to cut the taxes they pay, and demand cuts to public services and public employment.

The competitive drive to maximize profits and the private ownership of social means of livelihood are at the root of recurring booms and busts. Real capitalism (as opposed to theoretical) is inherently unstable. Individual enterprises can increase profits by cutting employment and wages, but when enterprises generally cut employment and wages, consumer income falls, markets stagnate and decline, overall profits decline. Selling shares that are losing value and buying those with higher rates of return can drive stock market booms, but writing off the value of real means of livelihood leads to unemployment and the decline of economies.

Supporters of capitalism look to new technologies to bring economic crises to an end. In the past, periods of decline were transformed into booms by new technologies such as steam-powered industrial machinery, the building of railways, electrification, the shift from coal to petroleum, plastics, mass automobile use and air travel. But the impact of new technology is unpredictable. The latest new technology, computerization, has actually been accompanied by declining real wages, stagnating global markets and lower rates of investment in real means of livelihood.

To revive markets, capitalists rely more on militarism and war. Purchased by governments, military manufacturing does not flood markets and drive down profitability as occurs with additional production of consumer goods. Military production — typically cost-plus and protected from careful public scrutiny — generates higher than average profits. War or its threat can justify massive government expenditures on research and development, which can give corporations access to profitable new technologies. When war destroys other countries' means of livelihood, it eliminates competition. It can give victors control of new markets and cheaper sources of supply.

Capitalists may increase their profits, but for most people war is anything but beneficial. For countries invaded and occupied, wars are catastrophes of death and destruction. For countries that have not become battlefields, war means repression, shortages, rising food prices, loss of trade relations, unemployment, conscription, the maiming and death of brothers, sons, daughters. From the 18th to the middle of the 20th century, war often appeared to benefit people in Europe, North America and the former British dominions. Control of the markets, supplies and surpluses of other countries made it easier for capital in the imperial centers to make concessions to unions and the poor at home. But now that capitalist property relations have been established in nearly all countries, war can have no net benefits. Since the 1940s every war and occupation, from Korea, to Vietnam, Somalia, Iraq, Afghanistan, Haiti and Libya, have come with costs that far exceeded benefits. Of course most of the costs have been borne by the people who were invaded or occupied, but the U.S. and its allies also suffered unacceptable casualties, faced growing hatred and accumulated trillions in public debt. The only tangible benefit went to capitalists who profited from provisioning the military.

8. Capitalism and the environment

The capitalist drive to maximize profits also explains the externalizing of environmental costs. Capitalism is a system that allows small minorities to profit at the expense of others. Private ownership of what are social means of livelihood allows capitalists to pass the real costs of industry to communities, workers, future generations and other species.

Capitalism began with enclosures, the dispossession of rural populations, the genocidal destruction of indigenous communities, as well as the near total destruction of walrus, sea otters, whales, North American bison and many other species. Twenty-first century capitalism is a world of private automobiles, sprawling suburbs, planned obsolescence and disposable products. Packaging often costs more than the products. Marketing budgets dwarf research and development. The manic, ever-expanding production and distribution of more commodities, the waste of labor and natural resources are systemic. Financial speculation generates more income than real innovation.

Now that the human population has passed six billion, it should be obvious that we inhabit a planet of finite resources. But population growth is not the problem. Human energy remains our most precious and underutilized resource. Once basic material needs for food, clothing, housing and healthcare have been met, human wellbeing depends less on consumption than on opportunities for education, employment, social participation and social recognition.

The problem is the systemic profligacy of capitalism. During the 20th century, soils, waterways and the atmosphere were polluted with industrial and agricultural chemicals. The expanding use of fossil fuels pushed atmospheric carbon dioxide to levels that dangerously increased global temperatures, acidified oceans and raised sea levels. Storms became more frequent and violent.

Science leaves little reasonable doubt that the burning of currently known reserves of coal, oil and natural gas will push atmospheric carbon dioxide levels past a tipping point, after which rising global temperatures will irreversibly undermine the conditions on which human life as we know it depends.

Despite the weight of evidence and the urgency of the problem, capitalism rests on the expansion of fossil fuel production and use.

Around the planet trillions of dollars are being spent to develop massive deposits of shale oil and gas. In Canada capitalist investment is focused on expanding oil production from tar sands. The promoters claim that these developments will create jobs. But the funds required to develop and transport that fuel will create far fewer jobs than would be produced if equivalent amounts were spent on the development of solar, wind and geothermal power. Far more jobs could be produced with investments in domestic employment for domestic markets, in the production and distribution of local agriculture, clothing, shoes and communications products. More jobs would be created by investments in childcare, elder care, social housing, public transit and other green infrastructure.

Capitalism prefers investments in fossil fuels because corporate profits now largely depend on cheap fuel. Equivalent profits cannot be made meeting actual human needs.

II — The Working Class and the New Commune-ists

In what relation do the new commune-ists stand to the working class as a whole?

We do not form separate parties opposed to other working-class parties. We have no interests separate and apart from those of the working class as a whole. We do not set up any sectarian principles of our own, by which to shape and mold the working-class movement.

The aim of new commune-ists can be summed up in one sentence: End minority rule and advance human wellbeing by abolishing capitalist entitlement.

We are distinguished from other working-class parties by this only:

(1) In the struggles of the working class of different countries we point out and bring to the front the common interests of the entire working class, independent of nationality and sectional interest.

(2) In the various struggles of workers against capitalism, we always and everywhere represent the long-term interests of the movement as a whole. These interests include economic democracy, environmental sustainability and global solidarity. We battle ideologies that divide us, especially racism, sexism and homophobia.

The working class now has the objective capacity to replace capitalism with economic democracy. Wage and salary workers are majorities nearly everywhere, but organized opposition to capitalism is largely non-existent. While we focus on single issues — wage rates, poverty, disparities, racism, sexism, or looming environmental crises — capitalist entitlement, the source of these problems, is left unchallenged.

Differences within the working class are real. Industrial, service and clerical workers can be subject to close and humiliating supervision while many skilled tradespeople, technical specialists, and professionals effectively control their labor time. Within countries, the best-off wage workers can be paid five or even ten times more than the lowest paid. Wage workers in countries with the lowest wages, can earn as little as one-fiftieth the pay of workers doing similar jobs in North America, the EU, or Japan.

Still, so long as we identify with what makes us different, we are playing a game that favors capitalist interests.

Working people will remain an incoherent mass so long as we divide ourselves by occupation, industry, gender, sexuality, ethnicity, language, country and mutual competition. The role of new commune-ists is to convince the working class everywhere that capitalism is the problem. No matter our occupation, our country, or our language, capitalists are in an unrelenting quest to maximize their profits by cutting our pay, employment, social entitlements, our rights to pensions, education and healthcare. To make matters even worse, capitalists continue to externalize environmental costs, threatening the future of our children and the livability of our planet.

But criticizing capitalism is not enough. We need an alternative that will better serve the interests of humankind. That alternative is economic democracy. When economic democracy is seen to be the alternative, we will have no need to look abroad for an already existing system to mimic. We can look within, to the already existing working class. The working class, already doing everything necessary for economic wellbeing, has the capacity to replace capitalism with economic democracy.

1. Economic Democracy

Economic democracy means replacing corporate ownership with social ownership, replacing capitalist title with equal human entitlement, and replacing master-servant relations with workplace democracy.

Replacing corporate ownership with social ownership means ownership by our communes — the counties, towns, cities, regions, provinces, states, nations and international communities we live in. The aim is to bring possession of enterprises as close to local communities as is practical. Residents would replace shareholders as the beneficial owners of enterprises. One person, one vote would replace voting based on the number of shares owned. All levels of governance — towns, cities, regions, states, provinces, federal governments and the international community — would engage in transparent economic planning.

Equal human entitlement means the right of all inhabitants to participate as equals in their communities' economic decisions. Replacing capitalist title with equal human entitlement would end the priority now given to private profit. Social planning would be motivated by employment opportunities, fair wages, social services and environmentally sustainable industrial activity. When everyone — including people working in tourism, organic farmers, mushroom pickers, parents, teachers, students, scientists, as well as industrial workers — have an equal vote in their communities' decisions, environmental concerns will be at the top of the order paper.

With workplace democracy, workers in all occupations — machine operators, maintenance people, administrative workers, engineers and managers — would democratically direct their labor time. Divisions of labor would continue, but hierarchies of power would be brought to an end. Communities may democratically decide that everyone who works regular hours should be paid the same. Or they may decide that wage differentials are needed to encourage people to further their education and advance their skills. Or they may decide that more dangerous or less agreeable tasks should be better paid. Whichever the choice, disparities will be far narrower than under capitalism.

Owning communities would control the policies and overriding practices of enterprises. They would appoint auditors and the chairs of enterprise boards. Workers in each occupation would elect their supervisors and meet with other occupations to direct day-to-day enterprise affairs. Capitalist control of means of livelihood, and minority rule more generally, would come to an end.

The supporters of master-servant relations will cry: "Who will take charge; without someone to crack the whip, people will goof off; universal laziness will overtake us." We respond by calling this a contemptible prejudice against people who actually do the work. Even under capitalism, where most work for the profit of others, people with work experience know that pretending to work is boring, stressful and mind numbing. Once workers are entitled to participate as equals in their communities' economic decisions, and entitled to take part in the democratic direction of their labor time, it will be obvious that people are working for their communities and themselves. No longer alienated from their labor time, workers will be committed to the work they have freely chosen to do.

An important part of what the capitalist system does is create the workers it needs. What kind of workers are these? Good consumers who think they're stupid, only care about themselves, hate unions and are scared of their shadow. Capitalism tries hard to create those kinds of workers. What kind of workers does economic democracy need? Pretty much the exact opposite of what capitalism needs — smart, thoughtful, creative, environmentalist, caring, willing to stand up for themselves and others. How do we create people like that? Through struggle. A critical part of economic democracy will be creating the people we need to run the system. Marx thought everyone is naturally creative, but that capitalism stunted it. For him a central point of socialism was to unleash people's creativity and that would only happen through struggle.

With equal human entitlement in an economic democracy, everyone's needs — food, housing, healthcare, education and basic income — will be met as a social right. Wages will provide additional income. Perhaps some will choose not to work. Why would that be a problem? Currently, in more prosperous capitalist countries, 30 percent of working-age populations are either unemployed or not in the workforce. When social labor is seen to be a right as well as a responsibility, more people will freely choose to be employed. Social labor will become voluntary social activity.

Capitalism makes it appear that the more we consume, the happier we are. But are we? Consuming has come to be a reward for the daily humiliation, stress and bullying of master-servant relations. Consuming more is beneficial so long as it actually meets our families' needs. But who really believes that working longer hours to make more money to purchase more disposable, unneeded and unhealthy consumer goods actually improves anyone's quality of life?

Given the choice, many people would prefer more leisure time. When economies are organized democratically in the interests of human wellbeing, regular working hours are likely to be shortened — perhaps to 24 hours a week, or 1,000 hours a year. Since communities and workplaces will be directed democratically, we cannot precisely predict what decisions will be made. We can predict that unlike capitalism, which is structured to create disparities, to entitle a few and disentitle many, economic democracy will be structured to serve the interests of all. When everyone has an equal right to participate in their communities' decisions and in the direction of their social labor, general wellbeing will take precedence. Instead of profits, communities will focus on general wellbeing, on providing each and all with the capacity to develop and advance their skills and opportunities. Social organization will aim to meet individual and social needs, while facing ecological problems directly and transparently.

2. Answering objections

Capitalists will say that replacing capitalist title with equal human entitlement is just another name for the expropriation of private property. We reply that capital is not legitimate private property. Capital comes from the surpluses generated by social labor. It appears as private property only because capitalist law gives a minority of wealth-holders the right to claim private ownership of the gifts of nature, socially produced assets and the net values produced by social labor.

Capital as it exists today comes from generations of exploitation of human beings and the gifts of nature. Capitalism began with enclosures, the driving of people from lands their ancestors had farmed from time immemorial. More capital was accumulated through the dispossession of indigenous people in the New World and the hunting and enslavement of Africans. Capitalist fortunes were made when imperial rulers in India and China declared lands private property, reducing peasants to landless day laborers. When crops failed they were left to starve as capitalists sold their produce where prices were highest.

Regardless, the supporters of minority entitlement will say: "Capital is legally acquired private property; it is the fruit of the labor of capitalists." That is rich. Capitalism mocks the right of people to the fruits of their labor. Under capitalism, majorities labor not for themselves, but for the profits of minorities. Those who work hardest get the lowest pay and are provided with the least for their declining years. Yes, capitalist law recognizes capital as private property. When capitalists make the rules, those rules benefit capital. In economic democracies, legislatures and courts will make and enforce rules that benefit all. When defenders of capitalism say that new commune-ists want to abolish private property what they really mean is that we want to abolish capitalist minority rule. To that we plead guilty.

The neo-conservatives who now dominate public policy nearly everywhere claim that private capital creates jobs and income; without capital invested in jobs, unemployment will rise; everyone will be poorer. But the truth is capitalist investment decisions are made to maximize profits, not to create jobs. To maximize profits, investment goes to labor-saving technologies or to where labor is cheaper.

Economic democracies will have surpluses and savings for investment. These will be held and allocated by community-owned financial institutions. Where proposed investments are uncontroversial, financial institutions and enterprises will bargain terms. Where there are disagreements or doubts, public hearings will be held and decisions will be made democratically. New enterprises that result will be community-owned and operated by the rules of workplace democracy.

Capitalist ideologues claim that without the focus on private profit there is no clear measure of the success of enterprises. Yes, profitability is a clear measure, but one that only benefits a small minority of shareholders. In an economic democracy communities would normally expect enterprises producing for exchange to generate enough revenue to cover costs and more, but the overriding goal will be human wellbeing. The measure of success of communities' economic decisions will be based on balances: on balancing employment opportunities with available labor; on balancing imports with exports; on balancing public revenues with needed public services, and on balancing industrial activity with the carrying capacity of environments.

Such social control, capitalists insist, would be the end of free markets. But free markets exist only in the imagination of ideologues. Markets comprised of numerous equal buyers and sellers, where all equally influence supply and demand, and all are equally aware of market conditions, are a myth. Under capitalism, markets are regulated and manipulated by dominant corporations that control marketing networks, supplies, patents, and spend massively on advertising. For capitalists, markets are free when capitalists unilaterally make the rules, when government regulations that inhibit their control are eliminated and workers are denied the right to bargain collectively. Free trade means the right of transnational corporations to direct international exchange for their private profit.

Let's be clear, we do not oppose production for exchange, or market forces. We, the consciously anti-capitalist working class, accept the benefits of fair markets. Changes in supply, demand and prices can assist communities in deciding where to allocate labor and resources. But our markets will be regulated democratically and transparently by all levels of governance. The aim will be to provide communities everywhere with access to international markets and supplies, while promoting local markets, local supplies and local employment. Our goal will also be to create new forms of community that break down the self-interest and mutual indifference that characterize capitalist exchange. Our goal will be to go beyond the narrow self interest of "I'll give you this, if you give me that" and "I only care about what I can get from you" to "From each according to their ability to each according to their need." If we can achieve that, we will also have achieved an end to the alienation that harms us all.

Supporters of capitalism will claim that our emphasis on the social relegates individuals to the background. In fact, it is capitalism that has made most individual labor impractical. Our goal is the democratic social ownership of means of livelihood that are already social. Where labor is individual, self-employment will be the rule. Individuals who gather, process, produce or exchange goods and services will be appreciated for adding to the wellbeing of communities.

Supporters of capitalism claim that economic democracy will end progress because it is capitalists who innovate. But this is rarely true. Bill Gates did not personally devise the computer operating software that made him one of the richest men in the world; he bought it for a relatively small sum. There is no evidence that capitalists are more likely to be innovators. On the contrary, individuals actually engaged in production processes are more likely to see new opportunities.

Economic democracy will inspire more people to look for innovations that are environmentally sustainable. Judgments as to what innovations are practical will not be made behind closed doors by venture capitalists, but transparently by community-owned financial institutions. If innovators fail to convince one community, they will have opportunities to pitch their proposals to other communities. Although innovators are unlikely to become fabulously wealthy, they could receive royalties, or be provided with employment more suited to their interests. And they would have the satisfaction of being successful innovators.

The supporters of wide disparities in income claim these are the source of great culture. Without the patronage of the super-rich, the greatest architecture, paintings, sculptures, music and science would not have been produced. Yes, when a tiny minority appropriates the wealth produced by entire communities, they have the means to define culture. But when communities control the surpluses produced by their social labor the arts will no longer be dependent on the patronage or charity of the super rich.

In a system of economic democracy, the arts will flourish. Art will become part of daily living and working. Its aim will be to make life more enjoyable, inspiring and beautiful. Artists will be freed to look at the human condition from distinctive perspectives. The elitist view that the masses will degrade culture is ridiculous.

It is capitalism that has made money the only standard of value. It promotes shallow consumerism. Its culture is fast food chains, cars, action movies, video games, professional sports, commodified sexual relations and the systemic disregard for environmental integrity and beauty.

Skeptics will say: "Why such confidence in the working class? Workers side with their employers on environmental issues. They support militarism and war. More workers probably supported the Tea Party than the Occupy Movement." Yes, capitalism encourages short-sighted, mean-spirited, competitive self-interest. It bombards individuals with advertisements designed to convince them that consumption is the essence of existence. It produces the consciousness of the people subjected to capitalist property relations.

Does the working class have the capacity to end capitalism and build economic democracy? The working class is the overwhelming majority and does everything necessary for human wellbeing. This question can be restated. Does humankind have the capacity to end minority rule? Are we doomed to forever being controlled by and in the interests of a tiny minority who are entitled to put their profits ahead of human wellbeing?

People who have spent their lives under capitalism are conditioned to accept the system's priorities. Economic democracy and movements to construct a world based on cooperation, democracy and equality will transform human consciousness. As community and workplace mobilizations against capitalism gain momentum, as working-class solidarity deepens and broadens, capitalism will lose the capacity to produce populations in its own image. As social entitlements expand, as democratic community ownership replaces capitalist title, as workplace democracy replaces master-servant relations, the self-centered competitiveness of capitalism will be replaced with community spirit, human solidarity, respect for nature, and the understanding that individual interest is tied to social and environmental wellbeing. People will come to deliberately, cooperatively and democratically produce their consciousness.

The sycophants of capitalism in universities, the media, churches and advertising, claim that private ownership of capital is the source of individual freedom, democracy and human happiness. We reply that freedom for capitalists means power over others. Capitalists have opposed democratic advances every step of the way.

3. 'Communist dictatorship'

But what about Communist dictatorship? The supporters of capitalism point to the USSR and China in the 20th century to claim that history shows the choice is capitalism or state tyranny. We look at the same history from the perspective of common people and conclude that while Communist Party states were undemocratic dictatorships, this is less a result of communism than of the relations these states had with the capitalist world.

The Bolshevik revolution began as a soldiers' revolt supported by the peasant majority, industrial workers and intellectuals. Czarist Russia had been an oppressive and abusive system that allowed officers to beat soldiers, and landlords to beat peasants. In 1914 Russia had the largest army ever assembled. Russian defeats and staggering casualties led to the collapse of the army and its reconstitution into revolutionary and counter-revolutionary forces. Most soldiers, being peasants, supported land redistribution. So did the Bolsheviks. Although they won the civil war, the Bolsheviks were surrounded by hostile capitalist powers that invaded, armed their internal enemies, embargoed their trade and demanded that Russia repay impossibly massive war debts to British, French and U.S. investors. Lenin, Trotsky and Stalin called themselves communists, but the state power they commanded relied more on armed force than on working-class support.

The Chinese Communist state can be explained by one hundred years of war and militarism. China was wracked with nearly continuous war beginning with the First Opium War with Britain in the 1840s. For 100 years imperial powers intervened militarily to establish protectorates and zones of influence. Civil wars raged between traditionalists and westernizers. Warlords battled to expand their territory. Japan invaded and occupied vast areas of traditional Chinese territory. Mao's People's Liberation Army, when it came to power, focused on freeing China from the imperial domination that had impoverished what had once been the world's largest economy. Chinese Communists unified the country and used state power to modernize the economy.

Certainly neither Russia or China ever tried to build economic democracy. At the time of revolution wage workers were a small minority in both countries. When one steps back from the rhetoric to look at the reality of the first five decades of both the Russian and Chinese revolutions one sees many similarities with the early decades of European capitalism. In fact, these economic systems should have been called "state capitalist" rather than "communist" or "socialist". They used the power of the state to accumulate enough capital to begin to compete with the rest of the world's capitalists. Certainly capitalist China now has an authoritarian centralized state. That is not an anomaly. Capitalists have long been the main beneficiaries of authoritarian states. Emerging in the transition from feudalism to capitalism, centralized states suited a system based on private capitalist title and master-servant relations.

When capitalist title is replaced with equal human entitlement, the goal will be sustainable human wellbeing. Governance will be based on democracy, transparency and dispersed, plural decision-making. Yet, while understanding the need for a new kind of state that does not stand above the people, the working class and new commune-ists do not share the hostility to government initiatives expressed by capitalist extremists and some anarchists. People with a social right to education, healthcare, pensions, housing, employment and minimum wages, unquestionably have more freedom. Even with democracy as limited as it is under capitalism, governments are less authoritarian, less arbitrary, less corrupt, less irresponsible and far more transparent than capitalist corporations. Because governments are not exclusively focused on shareholders' profits, they can focus on general interests. When economic democracy is the goal, working people will campaign for a broadening of social entitlements, as well as for open, transparent governance, and for public decision-making structures as close as practical to the people affected.

4. The working class: families, militarism and the state

In 1848 the supporters of capitalism charged communists with intending to abolish the family. This was a blatant falsehood. Family is at the center of working-class life. But the critics were partly right. In the years since, working people have succeeded in substantially reducing the authoritarian prerogatives and inequalities in families. Unions and labor-supported political parties have joined movements for public services, unemployment insurance and public pensions that made people less dependent on patriarchal family structures.

Working people have long campaigned for public education and for equal access to colleges and universities, as well as for universal public healthcare. Unions and community-based working people's organizations campaign for publicly funded pre-school care and for public elder care. Yes, families are the basic units of childrearing, but families exist within social networks. Without active social assistance, families, unless wealthy, are not equipped to do the job. Public education, public healthcare and public infrastructure such as waterworks, sewage systems, garbage collection and security services are needed to give families the means to properly prepare children for life as happy, productive, responsible adults.

In the past trade unions have adopted patriarchal positions, excluding women from membership and accepting lower pay rates for women. But in the late 19th and early 20th centuries unions and labor-supported political parties did mobilize support for women's suffrage and for campaigns to establish equal legal rights for women, including the right of married women to direct their own finances. As the proportion of women members rose, unions campaigned for equal pay for work of equal value and supported campaigns to provide women with a legal right to terminate pregnancy, and to protect partners in common-law and same-sex relationships. New commune-ists are at the forefront of battles in unions and in the wider community for an end to sexism.

Some unions in the past succumbed to racist and anti-immigrant sentiments. But since the 1970s most unions have supported civil rights campaigns. Labor-supported political parties have taken the lead in promoting legislation to end racial discrimination and discrimination against gays, lesbians, bisexuals and the transgendered. New commune-ists demand for all, regardless of background, ethnicity, sexual orientation, political belief or religion, that which we want for ourselves.

New commune-ists also understand, despite the daily propaganda to the contrary, that capitalism itself has become the greatest barrier to self-expression and creativity. Freeing all to develop their individual capacities requires more than individual will; it requires deliberate social initiatives. For capitalism, freedom belongs to the wealthy few. It reduces freedom and value to money, to how much one makes, what is most profitable. It warps self-expression and creativity. Human beings as a species will be freed to develop all their capacities only when basic needs have been made a human right, when all have equal access to employment opportunities, education and healthcare. All will be freed to be fully human only when everyone is entitled to a voice and equal vote in their communities' social decisions.

Capitalism will maintain its grips on means of livelihood, politics and mass consciousness so long as the working class fails to challenge militarism and war. Trade unions and working-class political parties supported their national governments in the European war of 1914-18. The internationalism that had been promoted by the Second Socialist International disappeared in a whiff of cannon fire. Tens of millions of young working men from Russia, Germany, France, Italy, Austria, Turkey, Britain, Canada, Australia, the U.S. and other countries were slaughtered and maimed in the mud, blood and filth of trench warfare.

A generation later, opposition to fascism provided more justification for warfare. Twenty-five million soldiers were slaughtered in the 1939-45 war; more than 40 million civilians lost their lives — over half in China and the Soviet Union. This war was followed by a generation of Cold War, ostensibly aimed against Russia. The consequence was hot, bloody war in China, Indonesia, Korea, Vietnam, Palestine and much of Africa as imperial powers used anti-communism to justify attacks on national liberation movements. At home unions and labor-supported political parties joined in anti-Communist campaigns, dividing unions and weakening working-class opposition to capitalism.

Working-class opposition to capitalism is incomplete so long as militarism and war are unchallenged. Armed force remains the foundation of minority rule. The death, destruction and hatreds generated by war become barriers to the international working-class solidarity that is required to end capitalism and build economic democracy. Force used against people abroad can be turned against working people at home.

The countries we live in — our national, regional and local governments — must be our overriding political focus. But limiting solidarity to within nations is dangerously divisive. Nationalism has been used to expand social entitlements. But nationalism is also used to divide workers, to direct the anger of the impoverished, unemployed and marginalized against others — foreign countries, immigrants, ethnic minorities — instead of against the system that is responsible for our common plight.

The power of capital is global. Economic democracy cannot succeed without becoming an international movement. This does not necessarily mean that we must have an international party. It does not mean we must wait for workers in other countries before we can challenge capitalism. But it does mean that we must come to consciously identify with all humankind. We must look for ways to act in solidarity with working-class struggles elsewhere. Where we take initiatives against capitalism, we must actively look for the broadest support. We must aim to build on working-class campaigns wherever they are.

New commune-ists do not go along with racist, sexist, militaristic, colonialist, or anti-environmentalist opinions. We respect fellow workers, but we take every opportunity to point out opinions that divide the working class only benefit the ruling class and are harmful to everyone else. It is not easy to overcome centuries of capitalist propaganda, but progress as a result of the women's movement, gay liberation and third world solidarity movements proves it is possible to change people's opinions.

5. The way forward

To end capitalism we must organize in workplaces and communities. In workplaces this means campaigns around immediate issues such as wages, hours of work and safety. We can organize by occupation, industry or sector. New commune-ists will relate these immediate issues to capitalism and to the alternative of economic democracy. We know that equal human entitlement cannot replace capitalist title until people in all occupations, men and women, blue collar, white collar, professionals, machine operators, service workers, the marginalized and the unemployed are united against capitalism. In our communities — local, regional, national and international — we will organize around the environment, social entitlements, employment opportunities, housing, basic income, education, healthcare and human rights. We will participate in all these movements and we will do more than just talk.

Where it is in the interests of workers to do so, we will support and organize strikes, picket lines and boycotts. We will approach these with the knowledge that in times of social confrontation strikes can be transformed into general strikes. General strikes can be transformed into the occupation of workplaces, the locking-out of the representatives of capital and the formation of workers' councils to democratically direct social labor.

New commune-ists, heirs to a 200-year history of working-class struggle, do not wait for revolutionary crises to oppose capitalism. We help mobilize workers against wage cuts, layoffs and outsourcing. We defend the right of communities to protect the integrity of their environments. We support the right of immigrants to be treated equally and oppose racism and sexism. We support electoral campaigns to win reforms that improve the quality of life for working people, the poor, the unemployed and the marginalized. To do this we rely more on mass mobilizations than on the goodwill of politicians or electoral parties.

One important lesson history teaches us is that capitalist property relations are not "natural" or inevitable. Human beings have satisfied their needs in a multitude of ways. Capitalism itself came about by replacing feudalism. The ideologues of feudalism claimed it was eternal and God-given, but it passed into history. The supporters of capitalism claim it is the "natural" order, the source of everything good: democracy, political freedom and rising living standards. But history makes it clear that the democratic rights we have now were won by common people, by unions, the poor, women, racialized minorities and colonized people. At every step capitalists opposed these movements. Capitalism is an economic system created by capitalists to suit their interests. Capitalists don't want markets free from rules. They want markets with rules made by capitalists, free from interference by others. At the beginning of capitalism its main enemy was feudalism, but now it's democracy.

6. Our agenda

The immediate priorities of workers can vary from country to country. New commune-ists will adapt agendas to local needs, but generally campaigns will focus on the following:

Repeal all laws that allow corporations to be treated as individual persons. Replace corporate ownership of land and resources with democratic social ownership by local, state/ provincial, national and international communities. Do the same with communications, transport and utilities. Transfer ownership of the media to cooperatives, communities, towns, cities, provinces, states and national governments. Public media, like other socially owned enterprises should operate with workplace democracy and be supervised by boards representative of the diversity of occupations and interests.

Legislate the right of all inhabitants to a voice and equal vote in their communities' social means of livelihood. Legislate the right of workers in all occupations to democratically direct their labor time.

Wherever practical replace production for exchange with production for human need.

Establish the right of people everywhere to basic needs including: food, housing, social employment, education, healthcare and a guaranteed annual income.

Establish steeply graduated income taxes and inheritance taxes. Expand property tax to include stocks, bonds and all other forms of wealth. Introduce financial transaction (Tobin) taxes. Keep tariffs low enough to broaden international trade, but high enough to encourage domestic production for domestic markets everywhere. Cut military spending to the minimum necessary to protect communities. Rely on transparent international agreements for security.

Support the rights of women everywhere to equal access to employment opportunities, to control their own bodies and to be freed from violence. Provide all families with access to childcare and eldercare. Oppose discrimination against gays, lesbians, bisexuals and the transgendered.

Campaign for electoral reforms that weaken the power of wealthy minorities to control and manipulate political agendas. Support and encourage unions to help finance anti-capitalist reforms. Campaign to establish the right of workers in all occupations to engage in collective bargaining and to be represented by unions of their democratic choice.

Support struggles of indigenous people for control of lands and resources in their traditional territories. Support their right to protect and advance their languages, customs and ways of life. Demand that treaty rights be respected and fully implemented. Campaign for the right of indigenous people to have equal access to education, healthcare and employment opportunities.

Support the rights of immigrants — documented and undocumented — to equal pay, equal social entitlements and the right to transparent due process.

Support campaigns to protect the environment and to immediately act to cut greenhouse gas emissions. Establish transparent environmental planning boards at all levels of government to redirect social employment away from the burning of fossil fuel. Provide alternate employment at equivalent pay and benefits. Provide all communities with the right to veto, by democratic vote, industrial activity in their territory.

67

For opponents of capitalism, reforms have come to have a bad name. Earlier in the twentieth century reforms were intended to improve the living conditions of workers without challenging capitalist title. In the last three decades reforms have come to mean increasing the wealth and power of capital at the expense of working people. The reforms we propose are intended to improve the living conditions of common people, to make human life sustainable and to methodically reduce capitalist privilege. As these reforms are implemented, economic democracy will progressively replace capitalist entitlement. In the end, the old capitalist society, with its classes and class antagonisms, will be replaced by an association in which the free development of each is the condition for the free development of all.

III — Our Relationship to Other Opponents of the Existing Social Order

1. Leninists

Leninists hold that a vanguard of the working class should form a political party that has the objective of taking state power by force of arms in the name of the working class. Leninists adhere to what they call democratic centralism, by which they mean that once a majority has voted, leaders must be trusted. New commune-ists argue death and destruction harm working-class interests and that history shows armed struggle gives the advantage to ruling classes. Where Leninists have taken state power, minorities continue to rule; over time capitalism is restored.

The all-knowing leadership is a seductive idea but it turns party members into followers who abdicate responsibility to others. This is what capitalism and its institutions encourage so it is no surprise that some workers have been seduced by it. Leadership is important and often not easy to explain, but when the goal is a world of human equality, democracy and cooperation, leaders cannot be above criticism or given extraordinary powers.

The working class does not need commanding officers, CEOs or chains of hierarchical command. The working class does need leaders dedicated to the common human interest. We need effective spokespeople who can rally broader solidarity. Such leaders will come forward as movements against capitalism expand. They will be men and women who respectfully listen to alternative views and are prepared to modify opinions while remaining implacably opposed to minority rule.

When few people oppose capitalism, those who do can view themselves as a vanguard, but new commune-ists expect that to be temporary. Without mass movements from the bottom-up a world of cooperation, democracy and equality will not be built.

When economic democracy is the goal, a centralized leadership is more likely to be an impediment. Effective strategies and tactics are more likely to grow out of numerous autonomous groups.

New commune-ists respect the work that Marxist-Leninists have done on behalf of the working class. Their history, like social democracy and anarchism, is part of our history, warts and all. Still we cannot ignore where Leninism went wrong. Militarism was viewed as a revolutionary force. The core Leninist belief led to the opposite of democracy, to repression, to mass murder and ultimate failure. What they built they called socialism, but a more accurate description is state capitalism. In most parts of the world, Leninist organizations have lost most of their influence. But in some countries they continue to have broad support. Insofar as Leninists advance working-class interests against capitalism, new commune-ists work with them.

2. Anarchists

Anarchists and Marxists have long been at loggerheads, divided by views on state power, authority and violence, and by sectarianism. Each group dwells on the deficiencies of the other and ignores the many areas of fundamental agreement. Official Marxism has long relied on authorities more than evidence. It is not surprising that those who call themselves anarchists are leery of those who used the state to suppress dissent, as in 20th century Marxist-Leninists states. Equally understandable is the disdain Marxists have for the anarchism that regarded the throwing of bombs as propaganda of the deed and now enjoys the destruction of property as political sport. Still, anarchists and Marxists often share a similar critique of capitalism and a vision of the future.

Those of us inspired by Marx do have a fundamental disagreement with anarchism. Anarchists oppose all states as instruments of repression. In the Communist Manifesto, Marx and Engels argued that the working class should take control of the state and begin building an alternative based on cooperation, democracy and equality. Yes, so long as property relations are based on minority entitlement, the state will remain an instrument of repression. But today the state, even under capitalism, has sometimes become an instrument used in the struggle for human wellbeing. Reforms have led governments around the world to provide social services such as education, pensions, unemployment insurance, income assistance, libraries and the security of persons as well as property. There should now be little doubt that states can be further democratized. The working class has the capacity to build polities that do not stand above the people. We begin by reorganizing our communities from the bottom up.

The disagreement between anarchists and Marxists on the state is more intellectual than practical. People who see themselves in the anarchist tradition work inside state structures and help mobilize people to defend social services. Some Marxists see most actually existing states as nothing more than tools of capitalist repression. There are non-violent anarchists and there are very violent Marxists. There are Marxists who have gained state power and used it to repress anarchists and other working-class dissidents, but there are also Marxists who have used state power to democratically and wisely advance the interests of the working class.

Three points: One, the measure of people's politics is what they do, not labels; Two, politics is seldom entirely black and white; Three, reasonable people who want to actually accomplish something focus on what unites, not what divides.

Identifying with the Marxist or anarchist tradition should not prevent people from working together. Putting aside historical differences, there is much more uniting than dividing us. For example, new commune-ists share with most anarchists a belief in empowering workers in workplaces and unions. New commune-ists share with many anarchists a belief in the importance of living in harmony with the environment. New commune-ists share with most anarchists a belief in multiple owning communities rather than one centralized state. New commune-ists share with many anarchists support for indigenous communities challenging settler colonial states.

New commune-ists are pleased to work with all those sisters and brothers who share a commitment to advancing the interests of the working class, regardless of some points of disagreement.

3. Social Democrats

Social Democratic, Socialist and Labor parties in most countries began as organizations of the working class, as electoral parties created and funded by unions. They have played a central role in winning reforms that have advanced democratic rights and expanded social entitlements. Today they often represent the actual views of workers and continue to hold the electoral allegiance of union members, but they are focused mostly on winning elections.

Because electoral gains in periods of extended capitalist growth depend on marginal shifts in prevailing opinions, social democratic parties have made a point of not rocking the boat. The trappings of political office easily seduce the leaders of labor-supported political parties. They welcome open supporters of capitalism into their ranks. They focus on one or a few issues and otherwise aim not to antagonize corporate power. If they succeed in winning political office either in their own name or in coalitions, they are happy to govern for what they view as all the electorate. In practice this means supporting and promoting dominant corporate interests.

Some social democrats continue to formally oppose capitalism; others advocate neo-conservative policies that weaken unions and reduce social entitlements. Some are little more than shills for war-mongering capitalists. It is on foreign policy that the failure of social democracy is most egregious. During the Cold War most social democratic parties supported capitalism against Communism. Perhaps some believed that the crimes of Stalin justified the Cold War. In practice anti-Communism led to support for imperialist wars against national liberation movements. It was used to justify the damage done to the democratic rights of people in the Congo, Guatemala and Iran, and the horrendous destruction poured on the people of Korea, the Philippines, Yemen, Algeria, Vietnam, Cambodia, Laos and many other countries.

New commune-ists do not object to electoral alliances or coalitions with capitalist parties if these are clearly intended to win support for reforms that benefit the working class. But we openly and continuously oppose policies that subordinate working-class interests to electoral considerations, or otherwise put the interests of capital ahead of human rights. We condemn militarism and war, whether openly racist or cloaked in the rhetoric of a responsibility to protect. At home militarism increases repression and strengthens capitalist interests. For people invaded, bombed or occupied, foreign military intervention is a catastrophe more destructive than domestic tyranny.

Until substantial numbers demand the right to vote for openly anti-capitalist political parties, new commune-ists will give their electoral support to existing labor-supported parties. Many supporters of these parties already object to capitalist entitlement but do not see a non-violent way to get rid of the system. We will work to convince them that economic democracy is a practical alternative that can be achieved through democratic mobilization for reforms that expand equal human entitlement, social ownership and workplace democracy.

Some social democrats claim that capitalists are required to deliver the government revenues needed for social programs. We respond that revenues capitalists invest are actually generated by social labor, by the working class. Capitalists have been rolling back social democratic reforms for at least 30 years. So long as they are free to direct socially produced surpluses in their private interests, capitalists will continue to do that.

Social democrats often justify support for the existing system by adopting Keynesian liberal ideology and claiming that the robber baron capitalism of the 19th century is part of history, that the system now is better described as market democracy. Who can reasonably believe that capitalist markets are neutral arbiters of contending class interest? Capitalism does not stand above class. It is a system of class struggle, of an unrelenting struggle by the one percent to maximize their profits at the expense of workers, First Nations, minorities, students, the marginalized and the poor. Defending capitalist entitlement means defending privatized public agencies, deteriorating social entitlements, widening disparities, worsening unemployment, declining real wages and an increasing reliance on repression and war. Accepting capitalism means supporting a system that gives private profits priority over environmental integrity. It means standing by as corporate oligarchs try to convince people that the profit-driven burning of fossil fuels cannot be connected to climate change.

4. Greens

Green parties now exist across the world. Most do not oppose the existing economic system and many see capitalism as part of the solution to environmental problems. Many Greens dismiss the working class as an appendage of unsustainable economic growth. But, in economies dominated by corporate advertising, the mass of the people cannot be blamed for consumerism. In a world where employment opportunities are controlled by capitalists, working people cannot be blamed for the work they do. People denied any ownership stake in their communities' lands and resources are not entitled to be vigilant against environmental damage. People who are left with no responsibility for anything but their families cannot be blamed for continuing population growth.

We do acknowledge that the environmental records of the Soviet Union and China were far from commendable. From its beginnings the Soviet Union focused on large-scale coal-fueled industry. Heavy industry polluted many of its cities. Draining the Aral Sea to irrigate cotton fields was a local and global disaster. Mao's policies were no better. China also looked to mega-projects and a future of coal-fired industrial development. Under the slogan "Man must conquer nature" the Great Leap Forward mobilized millions to denude forests to fuel backyard steel furnaces. Then, in a wrong-headed attempt to increase grain supplies, masses across China were mobilized to exterminate sparrows. The result? Insect infestations dramatically lowered harvests.

Like other environmentalists new commune-ists are appalled by the environmental damage done in the twentieth century by ruling parties calling themselves Communists. We go back to Marx, putting environmental destruction at the center of our opposition to capitalism. Working-class liberation, human equality and economic democracy would be hollow victories on a planet incapable of sustaining human life.

Few people are aware that Marx and Engels were far ahead of their time in drawing attention to the environmental damage that capitalist industrial growth would cause. In 1848, and over the rest of their lives, Marx and Engels described how the priority capitalism gives to private profit over human wellbeing would inexorably lead to ecological crises and catastrophes.

Some capitalists pay lip service to environmental concerns but capitalism is the problem. It makes waste and pollution profitable. A system driven to maximize profits cheapens labor and cheapens natural resources by externalizing environmental costs. Half and more of what the system produces is unnecessary or damaging to human wellbeing.

If individual wealth-holders, corporate executives and capitalist politicians propose measures to cut greenhouse gas emissions or reduce other kinds of pollution, new commune-ists will support their efforts. But we will continue to make the case that capitalism gives priority to private profit over environmental wellbeing. While green capitalism can be imagined, it is not the reality. Capitalists are concerned not with theoretical profitability, but with profits on existing investments. These rest on cheap energy from fossil fuels, on corporate petroleum-based agriculture, on petrochemicals and on disregarding the real costs of resource exploitation.

Wherever we can, new commune-ists will work with environmentalists, locally and globally. We see no division between the working class and environmentalists. Most environmentalists are in fact workers: electricians, clerks, teachers, machinists, laborers, technicians, accountants, university professors and people from every other occupation. New commune-ists will actively campaign to push unions to the forefront of battles for the environment.

Looming environmental crises require deliberate, cooperative human action. Capitalism based on narrow private interest and short-term profits is systemically incapable of providing that. Only a consciously anti-capitalist working class has the capacity and common interest to shift production for private profit to production for human wellbeing.

5. New commune-ists, unions and other working-class organizations

New commune-ists do not form hegemonic parties. That is not our goal. Our goal is the cooperative, democratic and egalitarian hegemony of the working class: rule by all for all.

Top-down centralized control, by strictly managing the message, may help political parties maximize electoral support.

But from a working-class perspective, short-term electoral gains based on the muting of opposition to capitalism undermine the capacity of the working class to mobilize against the system. Minority rule can only be ended by mobilizations of diverse sections of the working class in bottom-up local, regional, national and international initiatives.

Where reforms can be won that weaken capitalist title and strengthen economic democracy, new commune-ists participate in electoral coalitions, alliances and parties. But we oppose all attempts to subordinate working-class interests to those of political parties. Instead, we push and prod electoral parties that seek working-class support to openly campaign for our immediate and long-term interests.

New commune-ists do not distinguish ourselves from the working class, we are of the working class. We look to education and agitation, to union organization and to mass mobilizations for reforms that improve living conditions for common people, weaken the power of capital and bring us closer to economic democracy. We promote the interests of the working class through books, videos, magazines, newspapers, leaflets, blogs, local forums, teach-ins and in daily life. We actively promote opposition to capitalism in labor-supported political parties, in unions, communities, environmental organizations, international solidarity groups and student movements — everywhere that working people come together to promote our common interest.

New commune-ists are committed to the right of everyone to participate as equals in their communities' economic decisions. We support the right of rank-and-file members to participate in the determination of union policies and election of union officers. We encourage the broadest participation in policy discussions in labor-supported electoral parties. We aim to promote bottom-up solidarity, to win mass support for mobilizations that weaken capitalist title and expand social entitlements.

New commune-ists are there when local unions strike to improve their wages or working conditions, or simply to defend past gains. We are there when workers reject concessions and refuse to accept claw-backs and wage cuts. We are there when regional and national unions strike for pattern bargaining. We are there when a labor council or national union federation lobbies a government, rallies mass opposition, or calls a general strike to stop the latest attack on government programs, employment and workers' income. We are there when international labor federations act to build practical multinational links uniting occupations internationally. We are there when local unions and community groups mobilize against foreclosures, for social housing, for better healthcare or for debt relief.

New commune-ists join in campaigns for accessible unemployment insurance, for free post-secondary education and for the human right to a basic income. We take part in campaigns for free childcare and improved public education. We support collective bargaining rights for all public sector workers, including teachers and childcare workers.

We campaign for maternal and parental leave, for equality for women everywhere in the workforce and in the union movement. We support movements for indigenous rights, for the rights of temporary foreign workers and undocumented workers. We are there when unions and community groups mobilize opposition to militarism, foreign intervention and the occupation of other countries. We support the right of gays, lesbians, bisexuals and the transgendered to live in dignity and equality.

New commune-ists work to persuade unions to join with community groups to protect local and global environments. We actively campaign for transparent publicly funded plans to redirect industry away from reliance on fossil fuels. We advocate just transition policies that provide alternate employment at comparable wages for workers who lose employment for environmental reasons. We support the right of communities to veto industrial activity that could damage their local environment, a right that certainly applies to indigenous communities.

New commune-ists take every opportunity to point out that competitive private profit and unregulated capitalist markets are fundamentally incompatible with environmental integrity.

New commune-ists openly proclaim our aims and methods. Through generations of struggle around the world, common people have won some level of political democracy, free speech, freedom of association and the right to withdraw labor. We proudly use these hard-won gains to advance our cause. Let the capitalists tremble in fear of new commune-ism. The working class has a world to win.

Workers of all countries unite.

Epilogue

Another Conversation with Ernie

The following is an edited version of conversations that Gary Engler and Ernie Peshkov-Chow had about the New Commune-ist Manifesto after it was written.

GE — Why did you change the name to the *New Commune-ist Manifesto*?

EPC — Because commune-ist better explains what we believe in. Because too many people think "communist" means the people who ran the Soviet Union. Because you told me to.

GE — Did you learn anything from writing this? Stuff you didn't know? Or things that caused you to change your mind?

EPC — I learned a lot about the rotten shape our planet is in and how if we don't do something about it very soon, we're cooked. Literally. I mean I always thought of myself as an environmentalist, but writing this forced me to read and really think about it. I never realized how close we are to disaster. Basically, if we don't start reducing carbon emissions immediately, we're looking at a nightmare scenario for the planet. And capitalism won't fix it, can't fix it, because it is the problem. If we stay with our current economic system we're screwed. I guess what I'm saying is that before I wrote this manifesto I thought we had more time, but we don't. We've got to get away from capitalism's waste, from its always growing appetite for more profit and growth, from its irrational promotion of individual greed, from its externalization of social and environmental costs. We've got to get rid of minority rule and do it quickly.

GE — How do workers become environmentalists?

EPC — Lots of them already are. And most environmentalists are workers.

GE — That's a good slogan, but the truth is lots of workers are tied to jobs that depend on burning ever more carbon. How do you get workers building cars onside with getting rid of the private automobile? Or convincing people who build pipelines that we've got to stop extracting and shipping so much oil?

EPC — By talking to them, by showing them there's alternatives, by making them believe a better world is possible for them, their kids and grandchildren. People who build cars can build trains, subway cars or buses. People who build oil pipelines can build water lines or sewer systems. The truth is anyone who works is hooked to capitalism in one way or the other. People have to see the big picture, beyond what might appear to be their narrow self-interest at the moment. The job of the new commune-ist is to convince his or her fellow workers to look at our collective interest — the interest of humanity — and that is clearly being good environmental stewards. We say a good shop steward must also be a good environmental steward. Workers are better off in unions in which we show each other solidarity, sticking together for our mutual benefit. New commune-ists point out that the ultimate mutual benefit is a healthy environment. The values unions have always fought for are the values we continue to fight for. When we want for ourselves to have a healthy place to live, we wish for all to have a healthy planet.

GE — It's as simple as that?

EPC — Organizing a union is not simple, changing the system is one hell of a lot harder. But what's the choice? More of the same, which leads where? An environmental catastrophe with hundreds of millions of people dying? No future for our grandchildren? Workers' ultimate self-interest is in getting rid of minority rule, which means getting rid of capitalism and building a sustainable system of economic democracy.

GE — What would you like people to do once they've read the New Commune-ist Manifesto?

EPC — Start building an economic democracy with a focus on a sustainable environment.

GE — How practical is it for everyone in a community or workplace to have voice and vote?

EPC — Even corporations can have hundreds of thousands of shareholders. In theory each has a voice and vote. You don't need a post-graduate degree to figure out that the interests of people who are not allowed to participate in making decisions will be pushed to the back burner. So long as some have entitlements to means of livelihood and others do not, inequality and exploitation will be the result.

GE — If everyone is equally entitled, who will be in charge?

EPC — The common will. Decisions will be made following discussion, disagreement, compromise, consensus and, where necessary, majority votes. The point is that decisions will no longer be motivated by private profit, but by the common interest.

GE — Who would do the work if everyone's basic needs are met in any case?

EPC — We are social beings. We crave the approval of others. We take pride in knowing that we are doing our share. Workplace democracy would end the humiliation and alienation of work. With equal human entitlement, the required work week might be 24 hours. With workplace democracy, instead of being a crushing burden, work would be our main social life, a source of ongoing personal satisfaction.

GE — Isn't that the kind of utopianism criticized in the old Manifesto?

EPC — Marx and Engels criticized utopians for trying to get around the class struggle and for leaping into the future. The best of them tried to imagine a cooperative, democratic alternative to capitalism before that system had produced a working class with the capacity to replace minority rule with true democracy. Now that wage workers are the immense majority, and technology has made most of the drudgery in industrial labor unnecessary, we can see what a working-class alternative would look like.

GE — So how do we go about building economic democracy?

EPC — Think about the Manifesto for a little while, talk to your friends, family and co-workers. Get others to read it. But then, pretty darn quickly, start acting on it. The truth is we have the power to create ourselves by what we do, by how we struggle. So we've got to start doing the things that are necessary for us to become what we want to be.

EPC — The original Manifesto presumed that class struggle is violent. What do you think?

EPC — History tells us that ruling classes resort to violence if they think their privileges are threatened. Oppressed people respond with violence. That is likely to continue. But violence leads to hatred and divisions. When armed uprisings succeed, minorities seize power. When the goal is seen to be a world of human equality, democracy and cooperation, the working class will deliberately act to contain violence, relying on mass action and democratic political change.

GE — Your Manifesto departs quite a bit from what most people think were important principles in the original. Would it surprise you if some people thought you were betraying Marxism?

EPC — People can call me a traitor to Marxism all they want. It will only make me mad if they call me a traitor to the working class. I remember seeing a T-shirt back in the 70s with a picture of Marx holding up a sign that read: "I am not a Marxist." You asked me to produce an updated version of the Communist Manifesto reflecting what Karl and Freddy would write if they came back to life in 2013 and had a chance to study the past 165 years of working class history. That's what I did. If anyone wants to have an honest debate about my conclusions I am more than happy to show up any place, anytime. But if someone calls me names there's not much to say beyond "I know you are but what am I?" or ignore them like Mrs. Sawchuk told me all the way back in Grade 4. Besides, you tell me I'm not real so why should I care who I offend?

GE — Some people say history proves communism, socialism, anarchism, economic democracy — call it what you want — is not possible, that it's a dream which can never be realized. They say these ideal societies are not practical, that people can never learn to work together as would be required. They say people are naturally competitive.

EPC — That's a funny argument coming from capitalists since capitalism forces billions of workers around the world to work together for common purposes. That's what corporations do. They put lots of workers together in one place or many places and require them to cooperate. And the success of capitalism proves cooperation and working together are extremely efficient.

GE — Under managers who work for capitalists.

EPC — The point is people do work together. Workers do cooperate. To say they can't is stupid and flies in the face of human history. The question of how we manage that cooperation is entirely separate. Capitalists mostly hire other people to do their managing. They're called managers. If capitalists can hire managers why can't workers or communities?

GE — What are you saying?

EPC — The history of capitalism proves that working together and cooperation are both possible and efficient. It also proves that managers can be trained and hired. The history of modern capitalism proves capitalists are not needed. Except for their capital. That's the only thing they provide. And where do they get that?

GE — From owning things.

EPC — From exploiting us, which is another way of saying from accumulated profits or from loans, both of which they get because they own the economy. Both of which workers could get as well, if we stopped the exploitation and said we own everything that capitalists currently claim to own.

GE — Claim to own? You're saying capitalists don't really own their capital?

EPC — Workers made everything that earned the capitalists their profits that made them more profits and on and on. We'd own our means of production if we just stopped listening to them. The only useful thing capitalists do is replicate themselves and that's only useful to them and their closest friends.

GE — People say capitalists, in their search for profits, bring discipline, focus and efficiency to the system.

EPC — What does efficiency mean? Making more with fewer people. But do we need more? Can the planet afford more? Maybe what we really need is to make less with more people. Maybe we should all be working 20-hour weeks to get the things we really need and spend the rest of our time making art or gardening. Capitalism is incapable of even considering questions like that. It offers only two choices — growth or economic crisis.

GE — Do you really think workers would need to hire managers if we got rid of capitalism? Why couldn't we run things ourselves?

EPC — My point is that, even if we couldn't, we could at least run things the way capitalists do today. By hiring people. That's at a minimum. History proves that. But of course I believe we can run things. History shows it might take some time before we get good at it. Maybe we will need managers for a while.

GE — Do you think history is important?

EPC — Studying history is the only way to learn. If we do, it gives us confidence that what we're doing today might work.

GE — Do you think history is on our side?

EPC — In a way it is. I think history shows we can win. But it doesn't prove any particular outcome is inevitable. The world could end before economic democracy comes. History shows the actions of people determine the outcome. Today we don't have a lot of time to overcome the ecological rifts that human beings have created. We must get to it. We need to get rid of capitalism and replace it with a system that can repair the damage we have done. We know, from looking at the past, that human activity has destroyed the liveability of parts of the planet which were once very productive. We are on the verge of doing that again, but on an exponentially larger scale.

     GE — Are you hopeful or pessimistic?

     EPC — Pessimism leads to despair, retreat and inaction. I choose to hope, to act and to have fun. I try to be a realistic optimist with a sense of humor. I know one thing for certain: If enough of us act we will change the world. That fact alone will always keep me hopeful and willing to act.

Appendix

The Original

Communist Manifesto

By Karl Marx and Friedrich Engels

A spectre is haunting Europe -- the spectre of communism. All the powers of old Europe have entered into a holy alliance to exorcise this spectre: Pope and Tsar, Metternich and Guizot, French Radicals and German police-spies.

Where is the party in opposition that has not been decried as communistic by its opponents in power? Where is the opposition that has not hurled back the branding reproach of communism, against the more advanced opposition parties, as well as against its reactionary adversaries?

Two things result from this fact:

I. Communism is already acknowledged by all European powers to be itself a power.

II. It is high time that Communists should openly, in the face of the whole world, publish their views, their aims, their tendencies, and meet this nursery tale of the spectre of communism with a Manifesto of the party itself.

To this end, Communists of various nationalities have assembled in London and sketched the following Manifesto, to be published in the English, French, German, Italian, Flemish and Danish languages.

I — Bourgeois and Proletarians

The history of all hitherto existing society is the history of class struggles.

Freeman and slave, patrician and plebian, lord and serf, guild-master and journeyman, in a word, oppressor and oppressed, stood in constant opposition to one another, carried on an uninterrupted, now hidden, now open fight, a fight that each time ended, either in a revolutionary reconstitution of society at large, or in the common ruin of the contending classes.

In the earlier epochs of history, we find almost everywhere a complicated arrangement of society into various orders, a manifold gradation of social rank. In ancient Rome we have patricians, knights, plebians, slaves; in the Middle Ages, feudal lords, vassals, guild-masters, journeymen, apprentices, serfs; in almost all of these classes, again, subordinate gradations.

The modern bourgeois society that has sprouted from the ruins of feudal society has not done away with class antagonisms. It has but established new classes, new conditions of oppression, new forms of struggle in place of the old ones.

Our epoch, the epoch of the bourgeoisie, possesses, however, this distinct feature: it has simplified class antagonisms. Society as a whole is more and more splitting up into two great hostile camps, into two great classes directly facing each other -- bourgeoisie and proletariat.

From the serfs of the Middle Ages sprang the chartered burghers of the earliest towns. From these burgesses the first elements of the bourgeoisie were developed.

The discovery of America, the rounding of the Cape, opened up fresh ground for the rising bourgeoisie. The East-Indian and Chinese markets, the colonisation of America, trade with the colonies, the increase in the means of exchange and in commodities generally, gave to commerce, to navigation, to industry, an impulse never before known, and thereby, to the revolutionary element in the tottering feudal society, a rapid development.

The feudal system of industry, in which industrial production was monopolized by closed guilds, now no longer suffices for the growing wants of the new markets. The manufacturing system took its place. The guild-masters were pushed aside by the manufacturing middle class; division of labor between the different corporate guilds vanished in the face of division of labor in each single workshop.

Meantime, the markets kept ever growing, the demand ever rising. Even manufacturers no longer sufficed. Thereupon, steam and machinery revolutionized industrial production. The place of manufacture was taken by the giant, modern industry, the place of the industrial middle class by industrial millionaires, the leaders of the whole industrial armies, the modern bourgeois.

Modern industry has established the world market, for which the discovery of America paved the way. This market has given an immense development to commerce, to navigation, to communication by land. This development has, in turn, reacted on the extension of industry; and in proportion as industry, commerce, navigation, railways extended, in the same proportion the bourgeoisie developed, increased its capital, and pushed into the background every class handed down from the Middle Ages.

We see, therefore, how the modern bourgeoisie is itself the product of a long course of development, of a series of revolutions in the modes of production and of exchange.

Each step in the development of the bourgeoisie was accompanied by a corresponding political advance in that class. An oppressed class under the sway of the feudal nobility, an armed and self-governing association of medieval commune: here independent urban republic (as in Italy and Germany); there taxable "third estate" of the monarchy (as in France); afterward, in the period of manufacturing proper, serving either the semi-feudal or the absolute monarchy as a counterpoise against the nobility, and, in fact, cornerstone of the great monarchies in general — the bourgeoisie has at last, since the establishment of Modern Industry and of the world market, conquered for itself, in the modern representative state, exclusive political sway. The executive of the modern state is but a committee for managing the common affairs of the whole bourgeoisie.

The bourgeoisie, historically, has played a most revolutionary part.

The bourgeoisie, wherever it has got the upper hand, has put an end to all feudal, patriarchal, idyllic relations. It has pitilessly torn asunder the motley feudal ties that bound man to his "natural superiors", and has left no other nexus between people than naked self interest, than callous "cash payment". It has drowned out the most heavenly ecstacies of religious fervor, of chivalrous enthusiasm, of philistine sentimentalism, in the icy water of egotistical calculation. It has resolved personal worth into exchange value, and in place of the numberless indefeasible chartered freedoms, has set up that single, unconscionable freedom — Free Trade. In one word, for exploitation, veiled by religious and political illusions, it has substituted naked, shameless, direct, brutal exploitation.

The bourgeoisie has stripped of its halo every occupation hitherto honored and looked up to with reverent awe. It has converted the physician, the lawyer, the priest, the poet, the man of science, into its paid wage laborers.

The bourgeoisie has torn away from the family its sentimental veil, and has reduced the family relation into a mere money relation.

The bourgeoisie has disclosed how it came to pass that the brutal display of vigor in the Middle Ages, which reactionaries so much admire, found its fitting complement in the most slothful indolence. It has been the first to show what man's activity can bring about. It has accomplished wonders far surpassing Egyptian pyramids, Roman aqueducts, and Gothic cathedrals; it has conducted expeditions that put in the shade all former exoduses of nations and crusades.

The bourgeoisie cannot exist without constantly revolutionizing the instruments of production, and thereby the relations of production, and with them the whole relations of society. Conservation of the old modes of production in unaltered form, was, on the contrary, the first condition of existence for all earlier industrial classes. Constant revolutionizing of production, uninterrupted disturbance of all social conditions, everlasting uncertainty and agitation distinguish the bourgeois epoch from all earlier ones. All fixed, fast frozen relations, with their train of ancient and venerable prejudices and opinions, are swept away, all new-formed ones become antiquated before they can ossify. All that is solid melts into air, all that is holy is profaned, and man is at last compelled to face with sober senses his real condition of life and his relations with his kind.

The need of a constantly expanding market for its products chases the bourgeoisie over the entire surface of the globe. It must nestle everywhere, settle everywhere, establish connections everywhere.

The bourgeoisie has, through its exploitation of the world market, given a cosmopolitan character to production and consumption in every country. To the great chagrin of reactionaries, it has drawn from under the feet of industry the national ground on which it stood. All old-established national industries have been destroyed or are daily being destroyed. They are dislodged by new industries, whose introduction becomes a life and death question for all civilized nations, by industries that no longer work up indigenous raw material, but raw material drawn from the remotest zones; industries whose products are consumed, not only at home, but in every quarter of the globe. In place of the old wants, satisfied by the production of the country, we find new wants, requiring for their satisfaction the products of distant lands and climes. In place of the old local and national seclusion and self-sufficiency, we have intercourse in every direction, universal inter-dependence of nations. And as in material, so also in intellectual production. The intellectual creations of individual nations become common property. National one-sidedness and narrow-mindedness become more and more impossible, and from the numerous national and local literatures, there arises a world literature.

The bourgeoisie, by the rapid improvement of all instruments of production, by the immensely facilitated means of communication, draws all, even the most barbarian, nations into civilization. The cheap prices of commodities are the heavy artillery with which it forces the barbarians' intensely obstinate hatred of foreigners to capitulate. It compels all nations, on pain of extinction, to adopt the bourgeois mode of production; it compels them to introduce what it calls civilization into their midst, i.e., to become bourgeois themselves. In one word, it creates a world after its own image.

The bourgeoisie has subjected the country to the rule of the towns. It has created enormous cities, has greatly increased the urban population as compared with the rural, and has thus rescued a considerable part of the population from the idiocy of rural life. Just as it has made the country dependent on the towns, so it has made barbarian and semi-barbarian countries dependent on the civilized ones, nations of peasants on nations of bourgeois, the East on the West.

The bourgeoisie keeps more and more doing away with the scattered state of the population, of the means of production, and of property. It has agglomerated population, centralized the means of production, and has concentrated property in a few hands. The necessary consequence of this was political centralization.

Independent, or but loosely connected provinces, with separate interests, laws, governments, and systems of taxation, became lumped together into one nation, with one government, one code of laws, one national class interest, one frontier, and one customs tariff.

The bourgeoisie, during its rule of scarce one hundred years, has created more massive and more colossal productive forces than have all preceding generations together. Subjection of nature's forces to man, machinery, application of chemistry to industry and agriculture, steam navigation, railways, electric telegraphs, clearing of whole continents for cultivation, canalization or rivers, whole populations conjured out of the ground -- what earlier century had even a presentiment that such productive forces slumbered in the lap of social labor?

We see then: the means of production and of exchange, on whose foundation the bourgeoisie built itself up, were generated in feudal society. At a certain stage in the development of these means of production and of exchange, the conditions under which feudal society produced and exchanged, the feudal organization of agriculture and manufacturing industry, in one word, the feudal relations of property became no longer compatible with the already developed productive forces; they became so many fetters. They had to be burst asunder; they were burst asunder.

Into their place stepped free competition, accompanied by a social and political constitution adapted in it, and the economic and political sway of the bourgeois class.

A similar movement is going on before our own eyes. Modern bourgeois society, with its relations of production, of exchange and of property, a society that has conjured up such gigantic means of production and of exchange, is like the sorcerer who is no longer able to control the powers of the nether world whom he has called up by his spells. For many a decade past, the history of industry and commerce is but the history of the revolt of modern productive forces against modern conditions of production, against the property relations that are the conditions for the existence of the bourgeois and of its rule. It is enough to mention the commercial crises that, by their periodical return, put the existence of the entire bourgeois society on its trial, each time more threateningly. In these crises, a great part not only of the existing products, but also of the previously created productive forces, are periodically destroyed. In these crises, there breaks out an epidemic that, in all earlier epochs, would have seemed an absurdity -- the epidemic of over-production. Society suddenly finds itself put back into a state of momentary barbarism; it appears as if a famine, a universal war of devastation, had cut off the supply of every means of subsistence; industry and commerce seem to be destroyed. And why? Because there is too much civilization, too much means of subsistence, too much industry, too much commerce. The productive forces at the disposal of society no longer tend to further the development of the conditions of bourgeois property; on the contrary, they have become too powerful for these conditions, by which they are fettered, and so soon as they overcome these fetters, they bring disorder into the whole of bourgeois society, endanger the existence of bourgeois property. The conditions of bourgeois society are too narrow to comprise the wealth created by them. And how does the bourgeoisie get over these crises? On the one hand, by enforced destruction of a mass of productive forces; on the other, by the conquest of new markets, and by the more thorough exploitation of the old ones. That is to say, by paving the way for more extensive and more destructive crises, and by diminishing the means whereby crises are prevented.

The weapons with which the bourgeoisie felled feudalism to the ground are now turned against the bourgeoisie itself.

But not only has the bourgeoisie forged the weapons that bring death to itself; it has also called into existence the men who are to wield those weapons -- the modern working class -- the proletarians.

In proportion as the bourgeoisie, i.e., capital, is developed, in the same proportion is the proletariat, the modern working class, developed -- a class of laborers, who live only so long as they find work, and who find work only so long as their labor increases capital. These laborers, who must sell themselves piecemeal, are a commodity, like every other article of commerce, and are consequently exposed to all the vicissitudes of competition, to all the fluctuations of the market.

Owing to the extensive use of machinery, and to the division of labor, the work of the proletarians has lost all individual character, and, consequently, all charm for the workman. He becomes an appendage of the machine, and it is only the most simple, most monotonous, and most easily acquired knack, that is required of him. Hence, the cost of production of a workman is restricted, almost entirely, to the means of subsistence that he requires for maintenance, and for the propagation of his race. But the price of a commodity, and therefore also of labor, is equal to its cost of production. In proportion, therefore, as the repulsiveness of the work increases, the wage decreases. What is more, in proportion as the use of machinery and division of labor increases, in the same proportion the burden of toil also increases, whether by prolongation of the working hours, by the increase of the work exacted in a given time, or by increased speed of machinery, etc.

Modern Industry has converted the little workshop of the patriarchal master into the great factory of the industrial capitalist. Masses of laborers, crowded into the factory, are organized like soldiers. As privates of the industrial army, they are placed under the command of a perfect hierarchy of officers and sergeants. Not only are they slaves of the bourgeois class, and of the bourgeois state; they are daily and hourly enslaved by the machine, by the overlooker, and, above all, in the individual bourgeois manufacturer himself. The more openly this despotism proclaims gain to be its end and aim, the more petty, the more hateful and the more embittering it is.

The less the skill and exertion of strength implied in manual labor, in other words, the more modern industry becomes developed, the more is the labor of men superseded by that of women. Differences of age and sex have no longer any distinctive social validity for the working class. All are instruments of labor, more or less expensive to use, according to their age and sex.

No sooner is the exploitation of the laborer by the manufacturer, so far at an end, that he receives his wages in cash, than he is set upon by the other portion of the bourgeoisie, the landlord, the shopkeeper, the pawnbroker, etc.

The lower strata of the middle class -- the small tradespeople, shopkeepers, and retired tradesmen generally, the handicraftsmen and peasants -- all these sink gradually into the proletariat, partly because their diminutive capital does not suffice for the scale on which Modern Industry is carried on, and is swamped in the competition with the large capitalists, partly because their specialized skill is rendered worthless by new methods of production. Thus, the proletariat is recruited from all classes of the population.

The proletariat goes through various stages of development. With its birth begins its struggle with the bourgeoisie. At first, the contest is carried on by individual laborers, then by the work of people of a factory, then by the operative of one trade, in one locality, against the individual bourgeois who directly exploits them. They direct their attacks not against the bourgeois condition of production, but against the instruments of production themselves; they destroy imported wares that compete with their labor, they smash to pieces machinery, they set factories ablaze, they seek to restore by force the vanished status of the workman of the Middle Ages.

At this stage, the laborers still form an incoherent mass scattered over the whole country, and broken up by their mutual competition. If anywhere they unite to form more compact bodies, this is not yet the consequence of their own active union, but of the union of the bourgeoisie, which class, in order to attain its own political ends, is compelled to set the whole proletariat in motion, and is moreover yet, for a time, able to do so. At this stage, therefore, the proletarians do not fight their enemies, but the enemies of their enemies, the remnants of absolute monarchy, the landowners, the non-industrial bourgeois, the petty bourgeois. Thus, the whole historical movement is concentrated in the hands of the bourgeoisie; every victory so obtained is a victory for the bourgeoisie.

But with the development of industry, the proletariat not only increases in number; it becomes concentrated in greater masses, its strength grows, and it feels that strength more. The various interests and conditions of life within the ranks of the proletariat are more and more equalized, in proportion as machinery obliterates all distinctions of labor, and nearly everywhere reduces wages to the same low level. The growing competition among the bourgeois, and the resulting commercial crises, make the wages of the workers ever more fluctuating. The increasing improvement of machinery, ever more rapidly developing, makes their livelihood more and more precarious; the collisions between individual workmen and individual bourgeois take more and more the character of collisions between two classes. Thereupon, the workers begin to form combinations (trade unions) against the bourgeois; they club together in order to keep up the rate of wages; they found permanent associations in order to make provision beforehand for these occasional revolts. Here and there, the contest breaks out into riots.

Now and then the workers are victorious, but only for a time. The real fruit of their battles lie not in the immediate result, but in the ever expanding union of the workers. This union is helped on by the improved means of communication that are created by Modern Industry, and that place the workers of different localities in contact with one another. It was just this contact that was needed to centralize the numerous local struggles, all of the same character, into one national struggle between classes. But every class struggle is a political struggle. And that union, to attain which the burghers of the Middle Ages, with their miserable highways, required centuries, the modern proletarian, thanks to railways, achieve in a few years.

This organization of the proletarians into a class, and, consequently, into a political party, is continually being upset again by the competition between the workers themselves. But it ever rises up again, stronger, firmer, mightier. It compels legislative recognition of particular interests of the workers, by taking advantage of the divisions among the bourgeoisie itself. Thus, the Ten-Hours Bill in England was carried.

Altogether, collisions between the classes of the old society further in many ways the course of development of the proletariat. The bourgeoisie finds itself involved in a constant battle. At first with the aristocracy; later on, with those portions of the bourgeoisie itself, whose interests have become antagonistic to the progress of industry; at all time with the bourgeoisie of foreign countries. In all these battles, it sees itself compelled to appeal to the proletariat, to ask for help, and thus to drag it into the political arena. The bourgeoisie itself, therefore, supplies the proletariat with its own elements of political and general education, in other words, it furnishes the proletariat with weapons for fighting the bourgeoisie.

Further, as we have already seen, entire sections of the ruling class are, by the advance of industry, precipitated into the proletariat, or are at least threatened in their conditions of existence. These also supply the proletariat with fresh elements of enlightenment and progress.

Finally, in times when the class struggle nears the decisive hour, the progress of dissolution going on within the ruling class, in fact within the whole range of old society, assumes such a violent, glaring character, that a small section of the ruling class cuts itself adrift, and joins the revolutionary class, the class that holds the future in its hands. Just as, therefore, at an earlier period, a section of the nobility went over to the bourgeoisie, so now a portion of the bourgeoisie goes over to the proletariat, and in particular, a portion of the bourgeois ideologists, who have raised themselves to the level of comprehending theoretically the historical movement as a whole.

Of all the classes that stand face to face with the bourgeoisie today, the proletariat alone is a genuinely revolutionary class. The other classes decay and finally disappear in the face of Modern Industry; the proletariat is its special and essential product.

The lower middle class, the small manufacturer, the shopkeeper, the artisan, the peasant, all these fight against the bourgeoisie, to save from extinction their existence as fractions of the middle class. They are therefore not revolutionary, but conservative. Nay, more, they are reactionary, for they try to roll back the wheel of history. If, by chance, they are revolutionary, they are only so in view of their impending transfer into the proletariat; they thus defend not their present, but their future interests; they desert their own standpoint to place themselves at that of the proletariat.

The "dangerous class", the social scum, that passively rotting mass thrown off by the lowest layers of the old society, may, here and there, be swept into the movement by a proletarian revolution; its conditions of life, however, prepare it far more for the part of a bribed tool of reactionary intrigue.

In the condition of the proletariat, those of old society at large are already virtually swamped. The proletarian is without property; his relation to his wife and children has no longer anything in common with the bourgeois family relations; modern industry labor, modern subjection to capital, the same in England as in France, in America as in Germany, has stripped him of every trace of national character. Law, morality, religion, are to him so many bourgeois prejudices, behind which lurk in ambush just as many bourgeois interests.

All the preceding classes that got the upper hand sought to fortify their already acquired status by subjecting society at large to their conditions of appropriation. The proletarians cannot become masters of the productive forces of society, except by abolishing their own previous mode of appropriation, and thereby also every other previous mode of appropriation. They have nothing of their own to secure and to fortify; their mission is to destroy all previous securities for, and insurances of, individual property.

All previous historical movements were movements of minorities, or in the interest of minorities. The proletarian movement is the self-conscious, independent movement of the immense majority, in the interest of the immense majority. The proletariat, the lowest stratum of our present society, cannot stir, cannot raise itself up, without the whole superincumbent strata of official society being sprung into the air.

Though not in substance, yet in form, the struggle of the proletariat with the bourgeoisie is at first a national struggle. The proletariat of each country must, of course, first of all settle matters with its own bourgeoisie.

In depicting the most general phases of the development of the proletariat, we traced the more or less veiled civil war, raging within existing society, up to the point where that war breaks out into open revolution, and where the violent overthrow of the bourgeoisie lays the foundation for the sway of the proletariat.

Hitherto, every form of society has been based, as we have already seen, on the antagonism of oppressing and oppressed classes. But in order to oppress a class, certain conditions must be assured to it under which it can, at least, continue its slavish existence. The serf, in the period of serfdom, raised himself to membership in the commune, just as the petty bourgeois, under the yoke of the feudal absolutism, managed to develop into a bourgeois. The modern laborer, on the contrary, instead of rising with the process of industry, sinks deeper and deeper below the conditions of existence of his own class. He becomes a pauper, and pauperism develops more rapidly than population and wealth. And here it becomes evident that the bourgeoisie is unfit any longer to be the ruling class in society, and to impose its conditions of existence upon society as an overriding law. It is unfit to rule because it is incompetent to assure an existence to its slave within his slavery, because it cannot help letting him sink into such a state, that it has to feed him, instead of being fed by him. Society can no longer live under this bourgeoisie, in other words, its existence is no longer compatible with society.

The essential conditions for the existence and for the sway of the bourgeois class is the formation and augmentation of capital; the condition for capital is wage labor. Wage labor rests exclusively on competition between the laborers. The advance of industry, whose involuntary promoter is the bourgeoisie, replaces the isolation of the laborers, due to competition, by the revolutionary combination, due to association. The development of Modern Industry, therefore, cuts from under its feet the very foundation on which the bourgeoisie produces and appropriates products. What the bourgeoisie therefore produces, above all, are its own grave-diggers. Its fall and the victory of the proletariat are equally inevitable.

II — Proletarians and Communists

In what relation do the Communists stand to the proletarians as a whole? The Communists do not form a separate party opposed to the other working-class parties.

They have no interests separate and apart from those of the proletariat as a whole.

They do not set up any sectarian principles of their own, by which to shape and mold the proletarian movement.

The Communists are distinguished from the other working-class parties by this only:

(1) In the national struggles of the proletarians of the different countries, they point out and bring to the front the common interests of the entire proletariat, independently of all nationality.

(2) In the various stages of development which the struggle of the working class against the bourgeoisie has to pass through, they always and everywhere represent the interests of the movement as a whole.

The Communists, therefore, are on the one hand practically, the most advanced and resolute section of the working-class parties of every country, that section which pushes forward all others; on the other hand, theoretically, they have over the great mass of the proletariat the advantage of clearly understanding the lines of march, the conditions, and the ultimate general results of the proletarian movement.

The immediate aim of the Communists is the same as that of all other proletarian parties: Formation of the proletariat into a class, overthrow of the bourgeois supremacy, conquest of political power by the proletariat.

The theoretical conclusions of the Communists are in no way based on ideas or principles that have been invented, or discovered, by this or that would-be universal reformer.

They merely express, in general terms, actual relations springing from an existing class struggle, from a historical movement going on under our very eyes. The abolition of existing property relations is not at all a distinctive feature of communism.

All property relations in the past have continually been subject to historical change consequent upon the change in historical conditions.

The French Revolution, for example, abolished feudal property in favor of bourgeois property.

The distinguishing feature of communism is not the abolition of property generally, but the abolition of bourgeois property. But modern bourgeois private property is the final and most complete expression of the system of producing and appropriating products that is based on class antagonisms, on the exploitation of the many by the few.

In this sense, the theory of the Communists may be summed up in the single sentence: Abolition of private property.

We Communists have been reproached with the desire of abolishing the right of personally acquiring property as the fruit of a man's own labor, which property is alleged to be the groundwork of all personal freedom, activity and independence.

Hard-won, self-acquired, self-earned property! Do you mean the property of petty artisan and of the small peasant, a form of property that preceded the bourgeois form? There is no need to abolish that; the development of industry has to a great extent already destroyed it, and is still destroying it daily.

Or do you mean the modern bourgeois private property?

But does wage labor create any property for the laborer? Not a bit. It creates capital, i.e., that kind of property which exploits wage labor, and which cannot increase except upon conditions of begetting a new supply of wage labor for fresh exploitation. Property, in its present form, is based on the antagonism of capital and wage labor. Let us examine both sides of this antagonism.

To be a capitalist, is to have a personal title to wealth and also to have a social status in production, the right to command labor and to make economic decisions that effect entire communities. Capital is a social product, and only by the united action of many members, nay, in the last resort, only by the united action of all members of society, can it be set in motion.

When, therefore, capital is converted into common property, into the property of all members of society, personal property remains. It is only the social character of capital that is changed. Capital ceases to be private property. It loses its class character and becomes social property.

Let us now take wage labor.

The market price of wage labor under capitalism is the minimum wage, i.e., that quantum of the means of subsistence which is absolutely requisite to keep the laborer in bare existence as a laborer. What, therefore, the wage laborer appropriates by means of his labor merely suffices to prolong and reproduce a bare existence. We by no means intend to abolish this personal appropriation of the products of labor, an appropriation that is made for the maintenance and reproduction of human life, and that leaves no surplus wherewith to command the labor of others. All that we want to do away with is the miserable character of this appropriation, under which the laborer lives merely to increase capital, and is allowed to live only in so far as the interest of the ruling class requires it.

In bourgeois society, living labor is but a means to increase accumulated labor. In communist society, accumulated labor is but a means to widen, to enrich, to promote the existence of the laborer.

In bourgeois society, therefore, the past dominates the present; in communist society, the present dominates the past. In bourgeois society, capital is independent and has individuality, while the living person is dependent and has no individuality.

And the abolition of this state of things is called by the bourgeois, abolition of individuality and freedom! And rightly so. The abolition of bourgeois individuality, bourgeois independence, and bourgeois freedom is undoubtedly aimed at.

By freedom is meant, under the present bourgeois conditions of production, free trade, free selling and buying.

But if selling and buying disappears, free selling and buying disappears also. This talk about free selling and buying, and all the other "brave words" of our bourgeois about freedom in general, have a meaning, if any, only in contrast with restricted selling and buying, with the fettered traders of the Middle Ages, but have no meaning when opposed to the communist abolition of buying and selling, or the bourgeois conditions of production, and of the bourgeoisie itself.

You are horrified at our intending to do away with private property. But in your existing society, private property is already done away with for nine-tenths of the population; its existence for the few is solely due to its non-existence in the hands of those nine-tenths. You reproach us, therefore, with intending to do away with a form of property, the necessary condition for whose existence is the non-existence of any property for the immense majority of society.

In one word, you reproach us with intending to do away with your property. Precisely so; that is just what we intend.

From the moment when labor can no longer be converted into capital, money, or rent, into a social power capable of being monopolized, i.e., from the moment when individual property can no longer be transformed into bourgeois property, into capital, from that moment, you say, individuality vanishes.

You must, therefore, confess that by "individual" you mean no other person than the bourgeois, than the middle-class owner of property. This person must, indeed, be swept out of the way, and made impossible.

Communism deprives no man of the power to appropriate the products of society; all that it does is to deprive him of the power to subjugate the labor of others by means of such appropriations.

It has been objected that upon the abolition of private property, all work will cease, and universal laziness will overtake us.

According to this, bourgeois society ought long ago to have gone to the dogs through sheer idleness; for those who acquire anything, do not work. The whole of this objection is but another expression of the tautology: There can no longer be any wage labor when there is no longer any capital.

All objections urged against the communistic mode of producing and appropriating material products, have, in the same way, been urged against the communistic mode of producing and appropriating intellectual products. Just as to the bourgeois, the disappearance of class property is the disappearance of production itself, so the disappearance of class culture is to him identical with the disappearance of all culture.

That culture, the loss of which he laments, is, for the enormous majority, a mere training to act as a machine.

But don't wrangle with us so long as you apply, to our intended abolition of bourgeois property, the standard of your bourgeois notions of freedom, culture, law, etc. Your very ideas are but the outgrowth of the conditions of your bourgeois production and bourgeois property, just as your jurisprudence is but the will of your class made into a law for all, a will whose essential character and direction are determined by the economical conditions of existence of your class.

The selfish misconception that induces you to transform into eternal laws of nature and of reason the social forms stringing from your present mode of production and form of property -- historical relations that rise and disappear in the progress of production -- this misconception you share with every ruling class that has preceded you. What you see clearly in the case of ancient property, what you admit in the case of feudal property, you are of course forbidden to admit in the case of your own bourgeois form of property.

Abolition of the family! Even the most radical flare up at this infamous proposal of the Communists.

On what foundation is the present family, the bourgeois family, based? On capital, on private gain. In its completely developed form, this family exists only among the bourgeoisie. But this state of things finds its complement in the practical absence of the family among proletarians, and in public prostitution.

The bourgeois family will vanish as a matter of course when its complement vanishes, and both will vanish with the vanishing of capital.

Do you charge us with wanting to stop the exploitation of children by their parents? To this crime we plead guilty.

But, you say, we destroy the most hallowed of relations, when we replace home education by social.

And your education! Is not that also social, and determined by the social conditions under which you educate, by the intervention direct or indirect, of society, by means of schools, etc.? The Communists have not intended the intervention of society in education; they do but seek to alter the character of that intervention, and to rescue education from the influence of the ruling class.

The bourgeois claptrap about the family and education, about the hallowed correlation of parents and child, becomes all the more disgusting, the more, by the action of Modern Industry, all the family ties among the proletarians are torn asunder, and their children transformed into simple articles of commerce and instruments of labor.

But you Communists would introduce community of women, screams the bourgeoisie in chorus.

The bourgeois sees his wife a mere instrument of production. He hears that the instruments of production are to be exploited in common, and, naturally, can come to no other conclusion that the lot of being common to all will likewise fall to the women. He has not even a suspicion that the real point aimed at is to do away with the status of women as mere instruments of production.

For the rest, nothing is more ridiculous than the virtuous indignation of our bourgeois at the community of women which, they pretend, is to be openly and officially established by the Communists. The Communists have no need to introduce free love; it has existed almost from time immemorial.

Our bourgeois, not content with having wives and daughters of their proletarians at their disposal, not to speak of common prostitutes, take the greatest pleasure in seducing each other's wives. (Ah, those were the days!)

Bourgeois marriage is, in reality, a system of wives in common and thus, at the most, what the Communists might possibly be reproached with is that they desire to introduce, in substitution for a hypocritically concealed, an openly legalized system of free love. For the rest, it is self-evident that the abolition of the present system of production must bring with it the abolition of free love springing from that system, i.e., of prostitution both public and private.

The Communists are further reproached with desiring to abolish countries and nationality.

The workers have no country. We cannot take from them what they have not got. Since the proletariat must first of all acquire political supremacy, must rise to be the leading class of the nation, must constitute itself the nation, it is, so far, itself national, though not in the bourgeois sense of the word.

National differences and antagonism between peoples are daily more and more vanishing, owing to the development of the bourgeoisie, to freedom of commerce, to the world market, to uniformity in the mode of production and in the conditions of life corresponding thereto.

The supremacy of the proletariat will cause them to vanish still faster. United action of the leading civilized countries at least is one of the first conditions for the emancipation of the proletariat.

In proportion as the exploitation of one individual by another will also be put an end to, the exploitation of one nation by another will also be put an end to. In proportion as the antagonism between classes within the nation vanishes, the hostility of one nation to another will come to an end.

The charges against communism made from a religious, a philosophical and, generally, from an ideological standpoint, are not deserving of serious examination.

Does it require deep intuition to comprehend that man's ideas, views, and conception, in one word, man's consciousness, changes with every change in the conditions of his material existence, in his social relations and in his social life?

What else does the history of ideas prove, than that intellectual production changes its character in proportion as material production is changed? The ruling ideas of each age have ever been the ideas of its ruling class.

When people speak of the ideas that revolutionize society, they do but express that fact that within the old society the elements of a new one have been created, and that the dissolution of the old ideas keeps even pace with the dissolution of the old conditions of existence.

When the ancient world was in its last throes, the ancient religions were overcome by Christianity. When Christian ideas succumbed in the eighteenth century to rationalist ideas, feudal society fought its death battle with the then revolutionary bourgeoisie. The ideas of religious liberty and freedom of conscience merely gave expression to the sway of free competition within the domain of knowledge.

"Undoubtedly," it will be said, "religious, moral, philosophical, and juridicial ideas have been modified in the course of historical development. But religion, morality, philosophy, political science, and law, constantly survived this change."

"There are, besides, eternal truths, such as Freedom, Justice, etc., that are common to all states of society. But communism abolishes eternal truths, it abolishes all religion, and all morality, instead of constituting them on a new basis; it therefore acts in contradiction to all past historical experience."

What does this accusation reduce itself to? The history of all past society has consisted in the development of class antagonisms, antagonisms that assumed different forms at different epochs.

But whatever form they may have taken, one fact is common to all past ages, viz., the exploitation of one part of society by the other. No wonder, then, that the social consciousness of past ages, despite all the multiplicity and variety it displays, moves within certain common forms, or general ideas, which cannot completely vanish except with the total disappearance of class antagonisms.

The communist revolution is the most radical rupture with traditional relations; no wonder that its development involved the most radical rupture with traditional ideas.

But let us have done with the bourgeois objections to communism.

We have seen above that the first step in the revolution by the working class is to raise the proletariat to the position of ruling class to win the battle of democracy.

The proletariat will use its political supremacy to wrest, by degree, all capital from the bourgeoisie, to centralize all instruments of production in the hands of the state, i.e., of the proletariat organized as the ruling class; and to increase the total productive forces as rapidly as possible.

Of course, in the beginning, this cannot be effected except by means of despotic inroads on the rights of property, and on the conditions of bourgeois production; by means of measures, therefore, which appear economically insufficient and untenable, but which, in the course of the movement, outstrip themselves, necessitate further inroads upon the old social order, and are unavoidable as a means of entirely revolutionizing the mode of production.

These measures will, of course, be different in different countries.

Nevertheless, in most advanced countries, the following will be pretty generally applicable.

Abolition of property in land and application of all rents of land to public purposes.

A heavy progressive or graduated income tax.

Abolition of all rights of inheritance.

Confiscation of the property of all emigrants and rebels.

Centralization of credit in the banks of the state, by means of a national bank with state capital and an exclusive monopoly.

Centralization of the means of communication and transport in the hands of the state.

Extension of factories and instruments of production owned by the state; the bringing into cultivation of waste lands, and the improvement of the soil generally in accordance with a common plan.

Equal obligation of all to work. Establishment of industrial armies, especially for agriculture.

Combination of agriculture with manufacturing industries; gradual abolition of all the distinction between town and country by a more equable distribution of the populace over the country.

Free education for all children in public schools. Abolition of children's factory labor in its present form. Combination of education with industrial production, etc.

When, in the course of development, class distinctions have disappeared, and all production has been concentrated in the hands of a vast association of the whole nation, the public power will lose its political character. Political power, properly so called, is merely the organized power of one class for oppressing another. If the proletariat during its contest with the bourgeoisie is compelled, by the force of circumstances, to organize itself as a class; if, by means of a revolution, it makes itself the ruling class, and, as such, sweeps away by force the old conditions of production, then it will, along with these conditions, have swept away the conditions for the existence of class antagonisms and of classes generally, and will thereby have abolished its own supremacy as a class.

In place of the old bourgeois society, with its classes and class antagonisms, we shall have an association in which the free development of each is the condition for the free development of all.

III — Socialist and Communist Literature

1. Reactionary Socialism

a. Feudal Socialism

Owing to their historical position, it became the vocation of the aristocracies of France and England to write pamphlets against modern bourgeois society. In the French Revolution of July 1830, and in the English reform agitation, these aristocracies again succumbed to the hateful upstart. Thenceforth, a serious political struggle was altogether out of the question. A literary battle alone remained possible. But even in the domain of literature, the old cries of the restoration period had become impossible.

In order to arouse sympathy, the aristocracy was obliged to lose sight, apparently, of its own interests, and to formulate its indictment against the bourgeoisie in the interest of the exploited working class alone. Thus, the aristocracy took their revenge by singing lampoons on their new masters and whispering in his ears sinister prophesies of coming catastrophe.

In this way arose feudal socialism: half lamentation, half lampoon; half an echo of the past, half menace of the future; at times, by its bitter, witty and incisive criticism, striking the bourgeoisie to the very heart's core, but always ludicrous in its effect, through total incapacity to comprehend the march of modern history.

The aristocracy, in order to rally the people to them, waved the proletarian alms-bag in front for a banner. But the people, so often as it joined them, saw on their hindquarters the old feudal coats of arms, and deserted with loud and irreverent laughter.

One section of the French Legitimists and "Young England" exhibited this spectacle:

In pointing out that their mode of exploitation was different to that of the bourgeoisie, the feudalists forget that they exploited under circumstances and conditions that were quite different and that are now antiquated. In showing that, under their rule, the modern proletariat never existed, they forget that the modern bourgeoisie is the necessary offspring of their own form of society.

For the rest, so little do they conceal the reactionary character of their criticism that their chief accusation against the bourgeois amounts to this: that under the bourgeois regime a class is being developed which is destined to cut up, root and branch, the old order of society.

What they upbraid the bourgeoisie with is not so much that it creates a proletariat as that it creates a revolutionary proletariat.

In political practice, therefore, they join in all corrective measures against the working class; and in ordinary life, despite their high falutin' phrases, they stoop to pick up the golden apples dropped from the tree of industry, and to barter truth, love, and honor, for traffic in wool, beetroot-sugar, and potato spirits.

As the parson has ever gone hand in hand with the landlord, so has clerical socialism with feudal socialism.

Nothing is easier than to give Christian asceticism a socialist tinge. Has not Christianity declaimed against private property, against marriage, against the state? Has it not preached in the place of these, charity and poverty, celibacy and mortification of the flesh, monastic life and Mother Church? Christian socialism is but the holy water with which the priest consecrates the heart-burnings of the aristocrat.

b. Petty-Bourgeois Socialism

The feudal aristocracy was not the only class that was ruined by the bourgeoisie, not the only class whose conditions of existence pined and perished in the atmosphere of modern bourgeois society. The medieval burgesses and the small peasant proprietors were the precursors of the modern bourgeoisie. In those countries which are but little developed, industrially and commercially, these two classes still vegetate side by side with the rising bourgeoisie.

In countries where modern civilization has become fully developed, a new class of petty bourgeois has been formed, fluctuating between proletariat and bourgeoisie, and ever renewing itself a supplementary part of bourgeois society. The individual members of this class, however, as being constantly hurled down into the proletariat by the action of competition, and, as Modern Industry develops, they even see the moment approaching when they will completely disappear as an independent section of modern society, to be replaced in manufactures, agriculture and commerce, by overlookers, bailiffs and shopmen.

In countries like France, where the peasants constitute far more than half of the population, it was natural that writers who sided with the proletariat against the bourgeoisie should use, in their criticism of the bourgeois regime, the standard of the peasant and petty bourgeois, and from the standpoint of these intermediate classes, should take up the cudgels for the working class. Thus arose petty-bourgeois socialism. Sismondi was the head of this school, not only in France but also in England.

This school of socialism dissected with great acuteness the contradictions in the conditions of modern production. It laid bare the hypocritical apologies of economists. It proved, incontrovertibly, the disastrous effects of machinery and division of labor; the concentration of capital and land in a few hands; overproduction and crises; it pointed out the inevitable ruin of the petty bourgeois and peasant, the misery of the proletariat, the anarchy in production, the crying inequalities in the distribution of wealth, the industrial war of extermination between nations, the dissolution of old moral bonds, of the old family relations, of the old nationalities.

In it positive aims, however, this form of socialism aspires either to restoring the old means of production and of exchange, and with them the old property relations, and the old society, or to cramping the modern means of production and of exchange within the framework of the old property relations that have been, and were bound to be, exploded by those means. In either case, it is both reactionary and Utopian.

Its last words are: corporate guilds for manufacture; patriarchal relations in agriculture.

Ultimately, when stubborn historical facts had dispersed all intoxicating effects of self-deception, this form of socialism ended in a miserable hangover.

c. German or "True" Socialism

The socialist and communist literature of France, a literature that originated under the pressure of a bourgeoisie in power, and that was the expressions of the struggle against this power, was introduced into Germany at a time when the bourgeoisie in that country had just begun its contest with feudal absolutism.

German philosophers, would-be philosophers, and beaux esprits (men of letters), eagerly seized on this literature, only forgetting that when these writings immigrated from France into Germany, French social conditions had not immigrated along with them. In contact with German social conditions, this French literature lost all its immediate practical significance and assumed a purely literary aspect. Thus, to the German philosophers of the eighteenth century, the demands of the first French Revolution were nothing more than the demands of "Practical Reason" in general, and the utterance of the will of the revolutionary French bourgeoisie signified, in their eyes, the laws of pure will, of will as it was bound to be, of true human will generally.

The work of the German literati consisted solely in bringing the new French ideas into harmony with their ancient philosophical conscience, or rather, in annexing the French ideas without deserting their own philosophic point of view.

This annexation took place in the same way in which a foreign language is appropriated, namely, by translation.

It is well known how the monks wrote silly lives of Catholic saints over the manuscripts on which the classical works of ancient heathendom had been written. The German literati reversed this process with the profane French literature. They wrote their philosophical nonsense beneath the French original. For instance, beneath the French criticism of the economic functions of money, they wrote "alienation of humanity", and beneath the French criticism of the bourgeois state they wrote "dethronement of the category of the general", and so forth.

The introduction of these philosophical phrases at the back of the French historical criticisms, they dubbed "Philosophy of Action", "True Socialism", "German Science of Socialism", "Philosophical Foundation of Socialism", and so on.

The French socialist and communist literature was thus completely emasculated. And, since it ceased, in the hands of the German, to express the struggle of one class with the other, he felt conscious of having overcome "French one-sidedness" and of representing, not true requirements, but the requirements of truth; not the interests of the proletariat, but the interests of human nature, of man in general, who belongs to no class, has no reality, who exists only in the misty realm of philosophical fantasy.

This German socialism, which took its schoolboy task so seriously and solemnly, and extolled its poor stock-in-trade in such a mountebank fashion, meanwhile gradually lost its pedantic innocence.

The fight of the Germans, and especially of the Prussian bourgeoisie, against feudal aristocracy and absolute monarchy, in other words, the liberal movement, became more earnest.

By this, the long-wished for opportunity was offered to "True" Socialism of confronting the political movement with the socialistic demands, of hurling the traditional anathemas against liberalism, against representative government, against bourgeois competition, bourgeois freedom of the press, bourgeois legislation, bourgeois liberty and equality, and of preaching to the masses that they had nothing to gain, and everything to lose, by this bourgeois movement. German socialism forgot, in the nick of time, that the French criticism, whose silly echo it was, presupposed the existence of modern bourgeois society, with its corresponding economic conditions of existence, and the political constitution adapted thereto, the very things whose attainment was the object of the pending struggle in Germany.

To the absolute governments, with their following of parsons, professors, country squires, and officials, it served as a welcome scarecrow against the threatening bourgeoisie.

It was a sweet finish, after the bitter pills of flogging and bullets, with which these same governments, just at that time, dosed the German working-class risings.

While this "True" Socialism thus served the government as a weapon for fighting the German bourgeoisie, it, at the same time, directly represented a reactionary interest, the interest of German philistines. In Germany, the petty-bourgeois class, a relic of the sixteenth century, and since then constantly cropping up again under the various forms, is the real social basis of the existing state of things.

To preserve this class is to preserve the existing state of things in Germany. The industrial and political supremacy of the bourgeoisie threatens it with certain destruction -- on the one hand, from the concentration of capital; on the other, from the rise of a revolutionary proletariat. "True" Socialism appeared to kill these two birds with one stone. It spread like an epidemic.

The robe of speculative cobwebs, embroidered with flowers of rhetoric, steeped in the dew of sickly sentiment, this transcendental robe in which the German Socialists wrapped their sorry "eternal truths", all skin and bone, served to wonderfully increase the sale of their goods amongst such a public. And on its part German socialism recognized, more and more, its own calling as the bombastic representative of the petty-bourgeois philistine.

It proclaimed the German nation to be the model nation, and the German petty philistine to be the typical man. To every villainous meanness of this model man, it gave a hidden, higher, socialistic interpretation, the exact contrary of its real character. It went to the extreme length of directly opposing the "brutally destructive" tendency of communism, and of proclaiming its supreme and impartial contempt of all class struggles. With very few exceptions, all the so-called socialist and communist publications that now circulate in Germany belong to the domain of this foul and enervating literature.

2. Conservative or Bourgeois Socialism

A part of the bourgeoisie is desirous of redressing social grievances in order to secure the continued existence of bourgeois society.

To this section belong economists, philanthropists, humanitarians, improvers of the condition of the working class, organizers of charity, members of societies for the prevention of cruelty to animals, temperance fanatics, hole-and-corner reformers of every imaginable kind. This form of socialism has, moreover, been worked out into complete systems.

We may cite Proudhon's Philosophy of Poverty as an example of this form.

The socialistic bourgeois want all the advantages of modern social conditions without the struggles and dangers necessarily resulting therefrom. They desire the existing state of society, minus its revolutionary and disintegrating elements. They wish for a bourgeoisie without a proletariat. The bourgeoisie naturally conceives the world in which it is supreme to be the best; and bourgeois socialism develops this comfortable conception into various more or less complete systems. In requiring the proletariat to carry out such a system, and thereby to march straightaway into the social New Jerusalem, it but requires in reality that the proletariat should remain within the bounds of existing society, but should cast away all its hateful ideas concerning the bourgeoisie.

A second, and more practical, but less systematic, form of this socialism sought to depreciate every revolutionary movement in the eyes of the working class by showing that no mere political reform, but only a change in the material conditions of existence, in economical relations, could be of any advantage to them. By changes in the material conditions of existence, this form of socialism, however, by no means understands abolition of the bourgeois relations of production, an abolition that can be affected only by a revolution, but administrative reforms, based on the continued existence of these relations; reforms, therefore, that in no respect affect the relations between capital and labor, but, at the best, lessen the cost, and simplify the administrative work of bourgeois government.

Bourgeois socialism attains adequate expression when, and only when, it becomes a mere figure of speech.

Free trade: for the benefit of the working class. Protective duties: for the benefit of the working class. Prison reform: for the benefit of the working class. This is the last word and the only seriously meant word of bourgeois socialism.

It is summed up in the phrase: the bourgeois is a bourgeois -- for the benefit of the working class.

3. Critical-Utopian Socialism and Communism

We do not here refer to that literature which, in every great modern revolution, has always given voice to the demands of the proletariat, such as the writings of Babeuf and others.

The first direct attempts of the proletariat to attain its own ends, made in times of universal excitement, when feudal society was being overthrown, necessarily failed, owing to the then undeveloped state of the proletariat, as well as to the absence of the economic conditions for its emancipation, conditions that had yet to be produced, and could be produced by the impending bourgeois epoch alone. The revolutionary literature that accompanied these first movements of the proletariat had necessarily a reactionary character. It inculcated universal asceticism and social leveling in its crudest form.

The socialist and communist systems, properly so called, those of Saint-Simon, Fourier, Owen, and others, spring into existence in the early undeveloped period, described above, of the struggle between proletariat and bourgeoisie (see Section 1. Bourgeois and Proletarians).

The founders of these systems see, indeed, the class antagonisms, as well as the action of the decomposing elements in the prevailing form of society. But the proletariat, as yet in its infancy, offers to them the spectacle of a class without any historical initiative or any independent political movement.

Since the development of class antagonism keeps even pace with the development of industry, the economic situation, as they find it, does not as yet offer to them the material conditions for the emancipation of the proletariat. They therefore search after a new social science, after new social laws, that are to create these conditions.

Historical action is to yield to their personal inventive action; historically created conditions of emancipation to fantastic ones; and the gradual, spontaneous class organization of the proletariat to an organization of society especially contrived by these inventors. Future history resolves itself, in their eyes, into the propaganda and the practical carrying out of their social plans.

In the formation of their plans, they are conscious of caring chiefly for the interests of the working class, as being the most suffering class. Only from the point of view of being the most suffering class does the proletariat exist for them. The undeveloped state of the class struggle, as well as their own surroundings, causes Socialists of this kind to consider themselves far superior to all class antagonisms. They want to improve the condition of every member of society, even that of the most favored. Hence, they habitually appeal to society at large, without the distinction of class; nay, by preference, to the ruling class. For how can people when once they understand their system, fail to see in it the best possible plan of the best possible state of society?

Hence, they reject all political, and especially all revolutionary action; they wish to attain their ends by peaceful means, necessarily doomed to failure, and by the force of example, to pave the way for the new social gospel. Such fantastic pictures of future society, painted at a time when the proletariat is still in a very undeveloped state and has but a fantastic conception of its own position, correspond with the first instinctive yearnings of that class for a general reconstruction of society.

But these socialist and communist publications contain also a critical element. They attack every principle of existing society. Hence, they are full of the most valuable materials for the enlightenment of the working class. The practical measures proposed in them -- such as the abolition of the distinction between town and country, of the family, of the carrying on of industries for the account of private individuals, and of the wage system, the proclamation of social harmony, the conversion of the function of the state into a more superintendence of production -- all these proposals point solely to the disappearance of class antagonisms which were, at that time, only just cropping up, and which, in these publications, are recognized in their earliest indistinct and undefined forms only. These proposals, therefore, are of a purely utopian character.

The significance of critical-utopian socialism and communism bears an inverse relation to historical development.

In proportion as the modern class struggle develops and takes definite shape, this fantastic standing apart from the contest, these fantastic attacks on it, lose all practical value and all theoretical justifications. Therefore, although the originators of these systems were, in many respects, revolutionary, their disciples have, in every case, formed mere reactionary sects. They hold fast by the original views of their masters, in opposition to the progressive historical development of the proletariat. They, therefore, endeavor, and that consistently, to deaden the class struggle and to reconcile the class antagonisms. They still dream of experimental realization of their social utopias, of founding isolated phalansteres, of establishing "Home Colonies", or setting up a "Little Icaria" -- pocket editions of the New Jerusalem -- and to realize all these castles in the air, they are compelled to appeal to the feelings and purses of the bourgeois. By degrees, they sink into the category of the reactionary conservative socialists depicted above, differing from these only by more systematic pedantry, and by their fanatical and superstitious belief in the miraculous effects of their social science.

They, therefore, violently oppose all political action on the part of the working class; such action, according to them, can only result from blind unbelief in the new gospel.

The Owenites in England, and the Fourierists in France, respectively, oppose the Chartists and the Reformistes.

IV — Position of the Communists in Relation to the Various Existing Opposition Parties

Section II has made clear the relations of the Communists to the existing working-class parties, such as the Chartists in England and the Agrarian Reformers in America.

The Communists fight for the attainment of the immediate aims, for the enforcement of the momentary interests of the working class; but in the movement of the present, they also represent and take care of the future of that movement. In France, the Communists ally with the Social Democrats* against the conservative and radical bourgeoisie, reserving, however, the right to take up a critical position in regard to phases and illusions traditionally handed down from the Great Revolution.

In Switzerland, they support the Radicals, without losing sight of the fact that this party consists of antagonistic elements, partly of Democratic Socialists, in the French sense, partly of radical bourgeois.

In Poland, they support the party that insists on an agrarian revolution as the prime condition for national emancipation, that party which fomented the insurrection of Krakow in 1846.

In Germany, they fight with the bourgeoisie whenever it acts in a revolutionary way, against the absolute monarchy, the feudal squirearchy, and the petty-bourgeoisie.

But they never cease, for a single instant, to instill into the working class the clearest possible recognition of the hostile antagonism between bourgeoisie and proletariat, in order that the German workers may straightway use, as so many weapons against the bourgeoisie, the social and political conditions that the bourgeoisie must necessarily introduce along with its supremacy, and in order that, after the fall of the reactionary classes in Germany, the fight against the bourgeoisie itself may immediately begin.

The Communists turn their attention chiefly to Germany, because that country is on the eve of a bourgeois revolution that is bound to be carried out under more advanced conditions of European civilization and with a much more developed proletariat than that of England was in the seventeenth, and France in the eighteenth century, and because the bourgeois revolution in Germany will be but the prelude to an immediately following proletarian revolution.

In short, the Communists everywhere support every revolutionary movement against the existing social and political order of things.

In all these movements, they bring to the front, as the leading question in each, the property question, no matter what its degree of development at the time.

Finally, they labor everywhere for the union and agreement of the democratic parties of all countries.

The Communists disdain to conceal their views and aims. They openly declare that their ends can be attained only by the forcible overthrow of all existing social conditions. Let the ruling classes tremble at a communist revolution. The proletarians have nothing to lose but their chains. They have a world to win.

Proletarians of all countries, unite!